Eleven Mode

Eleven Modern Mystics

and the

Secrets of a Happy, Holy Life

Victor M. Parachin

Hope Publishing House
Pasadena, California

For information address:

Hope Publishing House
P.O. Box 60008
Pasadena, CA 91116 - U.S.A.
Tel: (626) 792-6123 / Fax: (626) 792-2121
HopePublishingHouse@gmail.com
www.hope-pub.com

Printed on acid-free paper

Cover design – Michael McClary/The Workshop

*Cover: Detail from "The Procession of the Just into Paradise" Icon
(1580-90, Sol'vychegodsk Museum of Art and History)*

Library of Congress Cataloging-in-Publication Data

Parachin, Victor M.
   Eleven modern mystics and the secrets of a happy, holy life / Victor M. Parachin.
        p. cm.

   ISBN 978-1-932717-25-9 (trade pbk. : alk. paper)
   1. Religious leaders. 2. Spiritual life. I. Title
   BL72.P27 2011
   200.92'2--dc23

                                        2011016726

Table of Contents

Introduction

We are surrounded by such a great cloud of witnesses (Heb 12:1).

It often happens that a person wishes to embark on a spiritual path but immediately doubts surface: Can I really do this? What are the first steps? Where do I start? Which way do I turn? Who can assist me? Such concerns can easily be swept aside by the simple realization that our world is teeming with spiritual mentors or, as the Bible has it, "We are surrounded by such a great cloud of witnesses." All we need to do is look at them, be inspired by them and permit them to show us the way.

This book relates the stories of eleven women and men who walked a spiritual path. Most of them come from a Christian background, but since spirituality cannot be contained and confined to any one faith, I have included lives from the Jewish, Buddhist and Hindu traditions as well. Though their religious and cultural backgrounds differ, they are all cut from the same cloth. This was something noted by the French philosopher Louis Claude de St. Martin: "All mystics speak the same language, for they come from the same country."

Everyone included in this book lived in the 20th century. Their history is our history. They are not legendary, distant, mythical figures, but are very much spiritual realists dealing with everything the 20th century brought them: war, genocide, discrimination, foreign occupation. In spite of experiencing the great evils and dark times of the 20th century, they continued to grow and evolve spiritually becoming beacons of hope and light on the planet. They are truly spiritual mentors for the rest of us. It is my hope that you will be informed, instructed and inspired by each one of them. —*Victor M. Parachin*

1

Dorothy Day

"Social Conscience of American Catholics"

Whatever I had read as a child about the saints had thrilled me. I could see the nobility of giving one's life for the sick, the maimed, the leper... But there was another question in my mind. Why was so much done in remedying the evil instead of avoiding it in the first place?... Where were the saints to try to change the social order, not just to minister to the slaves, but to do away with slavery? —Dorothy Day

When Dorothy Day died on November 29, 1980, her funeral was held at Nativity Parish, a church located in the poor neighborhoods of New York's lower east side. That day one of the Jesuit teachers at Nativity Parish School gave his class the morning off enthusiastically advising them: *Go to church today and see the funeral of a saint.* A remarkable comment given the fact that Dorothy Day, in her early years, had a series of lovers, got pregnant by one, had an illegal abortion, attempted suicide twice, was active in socialist and Communist movements. Nevertheless, in her lifetime Dorothy came to be viewed both as a saint and the living social conscience of the American Catholic church. As a young adult she began her quest for life's purpose, studying and proclaiming socialism. She ended as a Catholic highly influenced by socialist ideals. Prayer, justice, peace, solidarity with the poor were her ways of living out the teaching of Christ on love: *"My command is this: Love each other as I have loved you"* (Jn 15:12).

Dorothy was born November 8, 1897, in Brooklyn to John J. and Grace Day. Her parents were nominal members of the Episcopal church and had her baptized in that church. John was a newspaper reporter whose career meant many moves for the family. Dorothy spent her early years (1904-1906) in northern California where her father worked until the great San Francisco earthquake forced him to find another job. While living in Berkeley, Dorothy recalled a formative spiritual experience: "I remember we were in the attic. I was sitting behind a table, pretending I was the teacher, reading aloud from a Bible that I had found. Slowly, as I read, a new personality impressed itself on me. I was being introduced to someone and I knew almost immediately that I was discovering God." Intuitively spiritual, Dorothy was the only one of her family of seven to attend church, usually attending services by herself. When she was twelve she was baptized in the Episcopal church.

The family moved to Chicago in 1906. Feeling isolated from family and friends during those years, Dorothy turned inward, spending her time reading and writing. She attended the University of Illinois in Urbana where her commitment to writing deepened —as did her interest and involvement with pressing social issues: poverty, organized labor and war. Religious practice was not part of her life at that time. In her book, *The Long Loneliness*, she recalls being hostile to it: "I felt at the time religion would only impede my work. I felt it indeed to be an opiate of the people, and not a very attractive one, so I hardened my heart. It was a conscious and deliberate process."

Enticed by the radical social, cultural and political ideas prominent in New York, Dorothy dropped out of university in Illinois and moved there in 1916. She promptly found work as a writer for the *New York Call*, one of the nation's largest and most influential socialist daily newspapers. As a revolutionary journalist she covered labor movements, bread riots, unemployment, child labor laws, women's rights and protest marches on city hall. Quickly she began associating with the city's radical political and cultural thinkers. She met the Russian revolutionary Trotsky in New York and became a close friend of playwright Eugene O'Neill. Often she was at his side helping him deal with bouts of alcoholism. However, their friendship was not one-sided. O'Neill played an important role in Dorothy's eventual conversion to Catholicism.

As O'Neill listened to Dorothy talk of her evolving restlessness of spirit, and her feeling of something like a calling to do more and be more, he urged her to read St. Augustine's *Confessions*. There she came across Augustine's famous statement—one which resonated with her spirit: "You have made our hearts for yourself, O God, and they will never rest until they rest in you." This truth sank in and became a vital first step in her ultimate spiritual conversion.

Over the next decade, Dorothy drifted aimlessly. She parted company with her radical friends and eventually worked briefly as a nurse at a Brooklyn hospital where she met Lionel Moise, described as a "womanizing newspaperman." Their love affair resulted in Dorothy's becoming pregnant. She sought out an illegal abortion, an act which caused her considerable emotional suffering for many years. From nursing she returned to writing for small radically oriented newspapers. In 1920, she married the literary agent Berkeley Tobey, but the marriage ended a year later. She then moved to New Orleans where she worked as a journalist and during her sojourn there wrote a modestly successful novel, *The Eleventh Virgin* (1924).

For the first time in her life, she had financial resources and used them to move back to New York, buying a beach cottage on Staten Island. There she began living with Foster Batterham, a man she loved deeply and by whom she had a daughter, Tamar Teresa, born in 1927. This proved to be a pivotal turning point in her spiritual life and she chose to have her child and herself baptized into the Catholic church on December 28, 1927. Dorothy's spiritual transformation ended her relationship with Foster who could not understand nor appreciate her newly embraced faith. Although her conversion may have seemed sudden, it was actually the culmination of many experiences including:

- Late night visits to New York Catholic churches, possibly the result of reading Augustine.

- Fascination by the worship she experienced.
- Appreciation for the church's embrace of immigrants.
- Her 1922 Chicago experience where she lived with three young women, all of whom attended Mass regularly and made time for prayer daily. Their sincere piety made an indelible impression of Dorothy.

Being a new mother, becoming a single parent, and her embrace of a spiritual life drew Dorothy away from radical causes for a brief time. She spent time in prayer and discernment exploring how she could live out her faith as well as her commitment to social reform and justice. During these months of transition she took jobs in New York, Hollywood and Mexico—always living in poverty with the poor.

Dorothy also resumed her activity with social reform movements. In December 1932, she accepted a free-lance writing assignment for the Catholic publication, *Commonweal,* and went to Washington, DC to report on a Communist organized Hunger March. While there, she visited the National Shrine of the Immaculate Conception at the Catholic University of America, praying and seeking God's guidance for a way to open to use her talents and passions for the poor.

The answer to her prayer came quickly when she returned to New York and met Peter Maurin, a devout Catholic and social reformer who envisioned a society based on the teachings of Jesus where there were no divisions, as between workers and intellectuals. Maurin, a social philosopher who had the spirit of St. Francis, committed himself to simplicity and poverty. He often sought meals in skid-row missions, slept on the streets or wherever he found a bed. What little money he received, he spent on books or, more likely, gave it to the poor. He was convinced that radical social reform and the Roman Catholic faith could be united.

Dorothy was drawn both to his piety and to his passion for social justice. Their friendship and partnership quickly blossomed and Peter spent a great deal of time sharing his knowledge and insight about Catholic social philosophy with Dorothy, introducing her to important religious and social thinkers. Together they studied lives of the saints and the history of Christianity.

During their conversations, Peter outlined a three-step approach for transforming society: first, start a newspaper to promote socialist, Christian ideas; second, organize "houses of hospitality" to feed and clothe the hungry; and third, organize farming communes where people could live and work together for the common good. Since she was a journalist, Peter encouraged Dorothy to begin by starting a newspaper. It was this newspaper, *The Catholic Worker*, which launched the Catholic Worker Movement.

When they began *The Catholic Worker* as a monthly newspaper, they took bold and radical stands on current issues. First published in May of 1933 with a modest initial issue of 2,500 copies, within four months it had grown to 25,000 copies, and by the end of the year circulation was up to 100,000. By 1936 it was a nationally circulated Catholic newspaper reaching 150,000 readers. Parishes subscribed, often ordering bundles of 500 or more. Young activists took the paper, selling it on street corners. Soon the newspapers ideals were implanted deeply in the minds of many readers.

However Day was not content merely to write about socialist ideals. She wanted to back up her words with deeds, so she made part of their newspaper office into a "house of hospitality" which offered food and shelter for those in Depression-era poverty. It was the first of many such houses to be established. By 1936 there were 33 Catholic Worker homes around the country. Over the next five years, Day and the Catholic Worker Movement led the American Roman Catholic church in reform efforts. "What we would like to do is change the world," she declared. "Make it a little simpler for people to feed, clothe, and shelter themselves as God intended them to do. And to a certain extent, by fighting for better conditions, by crying out unceasingly for the rights of the workers, of the poor, of the destitute—the rights of the worthy and the unworthy poor, in other words, we can to a certain extent change the world; we can work for the oasis, the little cell of joy and peace in a harried world."

Dorothy's faithfulness to Jesus' message of love and her reading of Jesus' Sermon on the Mount led her to an uncompromising position as a pacifist. In 1936 Dorothy stated that she and the Catholic Worker were pacifist. The occasion which prompted that declaration was the Spanish Civil War. This brought her a barrage of criticism from church leaders and Catholic laity who had previously been attracted to her social ideals and activism. At the time, Catholics were strongly supportive of General Francisco Franco, a Catholic who eventually was victorious in the Spanish Civil War and became that country's head of state.

In spite of overwhelming questioning and criticism, Dorothy remained a staunch pacifist. When World War II erupted and American entered the conflict, she continued her pacifist stance which resulted in a steep decline of subscriptions to *The Catholic Worker*. Still, Day would not waver from her unshakable conviction that followers of Jesus could not and should not kill others. In her own way and in her own time, Dorothy was the Catholic equivalent of the nonviolent and pacifist principles of Mahatma Gandhi and Martin Luther King, Jr.

Furthermore, Dorothy's pacifism was completely consistent. She did not agree with the Christian "just war" teaching—the view that some wars are justified when certain moral conditions exist. Not did she agree with the Marxist views she subscribed to prior to her conversion, namely, the inevitable and violent overthrow by workers of the capitalist owners of industry. Her position of nonviolence was both resolute and uncompromising. For the January 1942 issue of *The Catholic Worker*—the first after the bombing of Pearl Harbor—Dorothy wrote: "Our manifesto is the Sermon on the Mount.... We will print the words of Christ who is with us always—even to the end of the world: 'Love your enemies, do good to those who hate you.'"

Because of her activism and outspoken criticism of American social structures, many within the American Catholic church became unhappy with her words and acts. Yet, her passion, sincerity and spirituality muted many critical voices. On one occasion New York's powerful and influential Cardinal Francis Spellman was asked to silence her. He had a well-earned reputation for being a vocal and steadfast social, political and theological conservative, yet in spite of the fact that his world view was the ideological opposite of Dorothy's, he was nevertheless startled and even offended by the suggestion he silence her. The cardinal had a simple, straightforward response as to why he would not do so; "She might be a saint." No bishop or cardinal would want to be remembered for censuring someone whom the church might later regard and canonize as a saint.

Although incredibly active and energetic throughout her life, Dorothy always struggled with depression. She described the pain of night: "My nights are always in sadness and desolation and it seems as though as soon as I lie down, I am on a tack of bitterness and pain. Then in the day I am again strong enough to make an act of faith and love to go on in peace and joy."

Because of her work among the poor, she frequently encountered women and men caught up in various addictions. Even these provided Dorothy with spiritual insights. For example, she commented on drugs and the things of God this way: "In the instance of drugs ... the need always seems to increase. How curious, that as in drugs so it is in the things of God: our capacity is always increasing. But do drugs lift the mind and the heart to God?"

Even though she worked with the poorest of the poor, Dorothy never passed judgment on them. In fact, she criticized Christians who did so saying: "[Being judged] is perhaps the greatest burden the destitute have to bear: the contempt, the judgment of others. 'If they would do this and this, they would get along better. If they would think this way, the way I think, if they did as I do, they would not have this mental breakdown.' There is always that assumption of superiority, of having in some way managed better, knowing better, than anyone else, in the attitude of those who help the poor. It is everywhere. It is among those who work in bureaus. It is in us who go to live with the poor and try to serve them. We intrude on them with our advice.... If we could only feed them, shelter them, clothe them without question, without assuming that we had all of the answers.

Dorothy never seemed to be discouraged by the waves of human need and misery which came as a never-ending surf. Author

Parker J. Palmer spent time at Catholic Worker and witnessed the enormity of their ministry. He asked Dorothy how she could "keep doing a work which never showed any results, a work in which the problems kept getting worse instead of better." Dorothy's answer was instructive and memorable for Palmer: "The thing you don't understand, Parker, is that just because something is impossible doesn't mean you shouldn't do it!"

Dorothy died on November 29, 1980, at Maryhouse, a house of hospitality for women. After a lifetime of living in poverty, Dorothy died penniless. There was no money set aside for her funeral. It was paid for the by archdiocese of New York. In 1998 she was nominated for canonization by Cardinal John O'Conner and in March of 2000, the Vatican began the process of considering Day for sainthood.

In the decades since her death, Dorothy continues to be held in high regard by those who study her life and contributions. In a recent article about her, writers Chris and Wayne Barrett offer these words of admiration and esteem for Dorothy: "Hostels were her cathedral. Rags were her vestments. Bread was her Eucharist, soup her wine. Her message made her the most influential and inspirational leader of Catholic outreach since Saint Francis of Assisi in the twelfth century, who, like her, called the church back to its 'communistic' roots of radical redistribution of wealth to insure that none were in need."

Reflection: Wisdom from Dorothy Day

I believe some people—lots of people—pray through the witness of their lies. Through the work they do, the friendships they have, the love they offer people and receive from people.

Love requires constant struggle. The less we work at love, the colder we become and the harder it is to receive the warmth of God's love. Religion is not just thinking—it is love. We shall be pierced.

When a person says he has done enough he has already perished. Some movement is always necessary—forward or backward. There is no vaca-

tion in the spiritual life.

As for ourselves, yes, we must be meek, bear injustice, malice, rash judgment. We must turn the other cheek, give up our cloak, go a second mile.

When we meditate on our Lord's life we are meditating on our own. God is to be found in what appears to be the little and the unimportant. Don't look back 1900 years. Look around us today.

Instead of fearing death, which changes nothing, we should fear life. That is because those who wish to enter heaven must be saints. Sanctity must be achieved in our lifetime.

If we wish the joy of heaven, we must cultivate a taste for it here.

One cannot be said to go to Mass to satisfy one's aesthetic sense. Or for the kicks. It is a duty and an obligation to come together in community to praise, honor, worship, thank the good Lord and to beg the strength to continue the daily round, bearing the daily sufferings of our human condition.

I have long since come to believe that people never mean half of what they say, and that it is best to disregard their talk and judge only their actions.

Love casts our fear, but we have to get over the fear in order to get close enough to love them.

The greatest challenge of the day is: how to bring about a revolution of the heart, a revolution which has to start with each one of us?

Action: How to Be like Dorothy Day

1. **Prepare yourself intellectually and spiritually.** Dorothy was a layperson and a woman who didn't hesitate to challenge positions held by those in Catholic hierarchy, including her own archbishop Cardinal Francis Spellman of New York. She was especially critical of their unrestrained patriotism and support of war. Dorothy didn't wait for the church to approve of her stand on nonviolence. She formed her positions after serious and thorough

intellectual preparation, studying the Bible (especially the Gospels), early Christian writings, papal statements, books and articles by theologians. In addition, she spent much time in prayer and meditation seeking spiritual insight, wisdom and direction from God.

2. Use all of your experience for the common good. Nowhere does Dorothy dismiss her preconversion or pre-Catholic life experiences. Rather, her early life events informed her maturing adult spirituality. She was able to use her past ordeals to shape present practices. For example, because Dorothy herself had an abortion, she was able to write a letter to a young, unmarried pregnant woman offering counsel, sharing her own pilgrimage and begging her not to subject herself to the suffering which she herself experienced as a result of the abortion.

3. Don't allow gender issues to hold you back. Dorothy lived before feminist and sexist issues became major public concerns, yet she was not constrained by gender issues. She was a professional woman, a journalist, an editor, author, single working mother, grandmother, social critic, pacifist, dissenter and the major leader of religious movement in a male-dominated church.

4. Be the incarnation of the divine for others. Dorothy often reminded people that God wishes to be manifested through us. "We must carry this glory in our lives so that when our neighbors touch us, they have contact with God." It's worth remembering that, for many people, the only link they have with God is through us.

5. Sometimes be in the company of people who don't agree with you. Dorothy wrote: "It is a matter of grief to me that most of those who are Catholic Workers are not pacifists, but I can see too how good it is that we always have this attitude represented among us. We are not living in an ivory tower."

6. Read spiritual writings. All her life Dorothy was an avid reader. She read Dostoyevsky, Tolstoy, Dickens, *plus* writings of a deeply spiritual nature: the *Psalms*, Augustine's *Confessions*, *The Imitation of Christ*—this 15th-century devotional book had a significant impact upon her when she was pregnant with Tamar.

7. Consider ways to simplify your living. Dorothy felt called to live a life of voluntary poverty. For her this meant living simply, wearing used clothing donated to Catholic Worker houses, traveling by public transportation, and having as few material possessions as possible. While you may not have Dorothy's calling toward voluntary poverty, perhaps you could consider ways to simplify your life, occasionally asking yourself: *Do I really need to buy this? Do I really need another possession in my life? Could the money I plan to spend be better used in support of someone who has far less than I do?*

8. Stand up for the values which are important to you. Dorothy was consistent and steadfast in maintaining her values: solidarity with the poor, nonviolence, pacifism, living in community. Conduct your own examination of conscience and life asking: *What values are important to me? Am I faithfully living by them? Am I an effective witness and example for others?*

9. Never give up on yourself. Keep in mind that Dorothy had an abortion. If she had given up on herself, if she had condemned herself saying, "I had an abortion. I'm of no use to God," church and society would have lost an important spiritual voice and presence. Never give up on yourself. God has a way of taking the broken pieces of our lives and creating a beautiful mosaic.

10. Don't take yourself so seriously and have a sense of humor. One day Dorothy was driven to Mass by a young man who was dating a Lutheran woman. Proudly he told Dorothy how he argued with her claiming the Catholic faith was superior to that of the Lutherans. "Did the Protestants have any saints?" he grilled her, answering "No." "Did the blessed mother visit any of them?" "No." As he went on and on, Dorothy recalls: "I felt like saying that Catholics needed them more."

Books by Dorothy Day

The Long Loneliness.
Loaves and Fishes.
From Union Square to Rome.

2

Thich Nhat Hanh

Engaged Spirituality

Meditation is not to escape from society, but to come back to ourselves and see what is going on. Once there is seeing, there must be acting. With mindfulness, we know what to do and what not to do to help. —Thich Nhat Hanh

"As the Nobel Peace Prize Laureate of 1964, I now have the pleasure of proposing to you the name of Thich Nhat Hanh for that award in 1967." So began a letter written on January 25, 1967, by Martin Luther King, Jr., to the Nobel Institute in Oslo, Norway. The world-renowned civil rights leader was promoting the cause of an obscure Vietnamese Buddhist monk unknown by most people in the West. In his letter Dr. King references the quagmire of the Vietnam War saying: "Thich Nhat Hanh offers a way out of this nightmare, a solution acceptable to rational leaders.... His ideas for peace, if applied, would build a monument to ecumenism, to world brotherhood, to humanity. I respectfully recommend to you that you invest his cause with the acknowledged grandeur of the Nobel Peace Prize of 1967. Thich Nhat Hanh would bear this honor with grace and humility."

Though Nhat Hanh would not receive the Nobel Peace Prize (no winner was selected that year) he would become known and loved worldwide. In the West, Nhat Hanh has become a Buddhist icon to thousands (including many Christians) who read his books, attend his workshops and visit his community in France. Among Buddhist leaders influential in Europe and North America, Nhat Hanh ranks second only to the Dalai Lama, the exiled spiritual leader of Tibet.

The person who would emerge to become the leading Buddhist teacher of his era was born in 1926 in the province of Quang Tri in central Vietnam. His birth name was Nguyen Xuan Bao, but he entered a monastery at age 16 and seven years later when he was ordained a monk he took the name Thich Nhat Hanh. *Thich*—an honorific title similar to "reverend"—is used by Vietnamese monks and nuns to indicate they are part of the Shakyamuni Buddhist association.

His becoming a monk coincided with the decline of French colonialism and the outbreak of the Vietnam War. As this escalated, Nhat Hanh, along with other Buddhists, began advocating what he called "engaged Buddhism" or what in the West could be classified as an engaged spirituality. He felt Buddhism had to have a practical impact upon people at all levels, from the poorest to the most powerful. Thus he and other associates worked rebuilding bombed villages, establishing schools and medical facilities. At the same time, Nhat Hanh was an outspoken advocate for peace and for peaceful, compassionate, humane solutions to differences. As a result, he came to the attention of Ngo Dinh Diem, president of South Vietnam, who considered Nhat Hanh, and others like him, subversive and sought to suppress and silence them.

As the war heightened, Nhat Hanh's peaceful opposition brought him recognition around the world. In 1966 he visited Pope Paul VI to gain the pontiffs support in ending the fighting. From there he traveled to the United States visiting with Defense Secretary Robert McNamara, Senator Edward Kennedy and other high-ranking U.S. government officials. He made contact with Martin Luther King, Jr., inspiring the civil rights leader to oppose the Vietnam War.

While abroad, the South Vietnamese government barred him from returning, making him a man without a country. In a letter to the Nobel Peace Prize committee, Martin Luther King wrote:

"Thich Nhat Hanh today is virtually homeless and stateless. If he were to return to Vietnam, which he passionately wishes to do, his life would be in great peril. He is the victim of a particularly brutal exile because he proposes to carry his advocacy of peace to his own people. What a tragic commentary this is on the existing situation in Vietnam and those who perpetuate it."

Nhat Hanh received diplomatic asylum in France where he continued promoting peace. In 1969 when the first peace talks seeking an end to the Vietnam War began in Paris, Nhat Hanh attended as a leader of a Vietnamese Buddhist delegation. In the United States, Nhat Hanh studied religion at Princeton University, was a professor at Columbia University and lectured at Cornell University.

When the South Vietnamese government fell to Communist forces in 1975, he led rescue efforts to aid fleeing refugees and sponsored programs supporting orphans within the country. The Communist government refused permission for Nhat Hanh to return. Exile was difficult for him. "In the beginning, I missed my country very much," he told a reporter. "I used to dream of going back. But now I feel I am home. Although I have been away for more than 30 years, my books, my tapes, have found a way back to Vietnam. Many friends of ours visit Vietnam from Australia, from Europe, report to me that my presence in Vietnam is very tangible, very real. So, I don't suffer because I cannot go home."

Nevertheless, the Vietnam War caused Nhat Hanh great suffering. He saw his country destroyed by war, countless people killed and injured, and experienced the loss of close friends. In 1967 while in Paris, he learned that one of his associates—a young woman named Nhat Chi Mai—immolated herself in front of the Tu Nghiem pagoda in Saigon protesting the war. Soon after, he received word that another friend, Thanh Van, was killed by an American military truck. Thanh Van was like a brother to Nhat Hanh. Overwhelmed with grief, Nhat Hanh retreated to his room for more than two months.

In spite of the great suffering the people of Vietnam were experiencing, Nhat Hanh continued to speak and act out of hope.

After he settled in France, Nhat Hanh began to welcome Vietnamese refugees. When the numbers began increasing, swamping his small hermitage, Nhat Hanh managed to purchase two abandoned farms in southwest France where he established Plum Village which has become his permanent home. There refugees were welcomed and permitted to stay until they were ready to enter French society. Nhat Hanh did not insist on any monastic disciplines for the refugees, but they were expected to help grow and harvest crops on the land and assist with his month-long summer retreats. His objective was simply to help refugees heal from the wounds of war while making a living in a safe, accepting community.

Ironically, exile served only to deepen Nhat Hanh's influence and popularity, not only in his homeland but around the world. He founded three monasteries in the U.S. and one in France and taught tens of thousands his concepts of "engaged Buddhism," which emphasizes meditation, peace and social justice. He has published over a hundred books which have sold 1.5 million copies. When not traveling, Nhat Hanh is back at Plum Village where hundreds of visitors come each year, almost like pilgrims, to spend time with Nhat Hanh absorbing his teaching.

One of his early and most influential books was *The Miracle of Mindfulness,* originally written as a long letter to a Buddhist Brother Quang in 1974 which contains the essence of his spiritual philosophy of "mindfulness." In this tract Nhat Hanh encouraged Brother Quang and others working in Vietnam during those dark, violent, turbulent times to focus upon their breathing. He reminded them to follow their breath to nourish and maintain calm mindfulness, even in the midst of brutal and often inhumane conditions. One of his famous meditations is simply these two sentences: "Breathing in I calm my body. Breathing out I smile."

Breath control and mindfulness are inseparably linked in this book where he notes: "You should know how to breathe to maintain mindfulness, as breathing is a natural and extremely effective tool which can prevent dispersion. Breath is the bridge which connects life to consciousness, which unites your body to your thoughts. Whenever your mind becomes scattered, use your breath as the means to take hold of your mind again."

Nhat Hanh's spiritual approach is immensely practical and embraces all aspects of daily life. For example, in his book, *Touching Peace*, Hanh, writing to couples and families, stresses the importance of mindful living together. "When we try to grow flowers, if the flowers do not grow well, we do not blame or argue with them. We blame ourselves for not taking care of them well. Our partner is a flower. If we take care of her well, she will grow beautifully. If we take care of her poorly, she will wither." His mindfulness spirituality is applied to even the mundane task of washing dishes.

This lesson was learned by American author and peace activist Jim Forest. Nhat Hanh tells of Forest visiting him and enjoying a meal together where he explained to Forest that his custom was to wash dishes after the evening meal but before the tea drinking ritual which followed dinner. When Forest offered to do the dish washing, Nhat Hanh said: "Go ahead, but if you wash the dishes you must know the way to wash them." Forest was both confused and intrigued. Nhat Hanh elaborated: "There are two ways to wash dishes. The first is to wash the dishes in order to have clean dishes and the second is to wash the dishes in order to wash the dishes. Choose the second way." With humor, Nhat Hanh adds that "from then on Jim knew how to wash dishes. I transferred the responsibility to him for an entire week." This lesson is a vital aspect of Nhat Hanh's mindfulness approach to life: *when walking, walk; when sitting, sit; when eating, eat; when washing, wash.*

His teachings and his books offer a wide variety of practical meditation exercises which can be applied throughout one's day and life. Some examples include: a half-smile meditation upon awaking each morning; a half-smile meditation when irritated; mindfulness while making tea or washing dishes and clothing; a meditation for house cleaning and bathing; a meditation for grieving the death of a loved one; a meditation on compassion for a person one hates or despises "the most." Nhat Hanh believes there is no aspect of life which cannot be responded to with mindfulness and compassion.

To help others wanting to follow the path of "engaged Buddhism" or an engaged spirituality, Nhat Hanh offers these 14 precepts to abide by: (although they are condensed here, a full development of these principles can be found in his book *Interbeing: Fourteen Guidelines For Engaged Buddhism.*)

1. Do not be idolatrous about or bound to any doctrine, theory or ideology, even Buddhist ones. All systems of thought are guiding means; they are not absolute truth.

2. Do not think that the knowledge you presently possess is changeless, absolute truth. Avoid being narrow-minded and bound to present views. Learn and practice non-attachment from views in order to be open to receive others viewpoints. Truth is found in life and not merely in conceptual knowledge. Be ready to learn throughout your entire life and observe reality in yourself and in the world at all times.

3. Do not force others, including children, by any means whatsoever, to adopt your views, whether by authority, threat, money, propaganda or even education. However, through compassionate dialogue, help others renounce fanaticism and narrowness.

4. Do not avoid contact with suffering or close your eyes before suffering. Do not lose awareness of the existence of suffering in the life of the world. Find ways to be with those who are suffering by all means, including personal contact and visits, images, sound. By such means, awaken yourself and others to the reality of suffering in the world.

5. Do not accumulate wealth while millions are hungry. Do not take as the aim of your life fame, profit, wealth or sensual pleasure. Live simply and share time, energy and material resources with those who are in need.

6. Do not maintain anger or hatred. As soon as anger and hatred arise, practice the meditation on compassion in order to deeply understand the persons who have caused anger and hatred. Learn to look at other beings with the eyes of compassion.

7. Do not lose yourself in dispersion (mindlessness) and in your surroundings. Learn to practice breathing in order to regain composure of body and mind, to practice mindfulness and develop

concentration and understanding.

8. Do not utter words that can create discord and cause community to break. Make every effort to reconcile and resolve all conflicts, however small.

9. Do not say untruthful things for the sake of personal interest or to impress people. Do not utter words that cause diversion and hatred. Do not spread news that you do not know to be certain. Do not criticize or condemn things you are not sure of. Always speak truthfully and constructively. Have the courage to speak out about situations of injustice, even when doing so may threaten your own safety.

10. Do not use the Buddhist (or any spiritual) community for personal gain or profit, or transform your community into a political party. A religious community should, however, take a clear stand against oppression and injustice and should strive to change the situation without engaging in partisan conflicts.

11. Do not live with a vocation that is harmful to humans and nature. Do not invest in companies that deprive others of their chance to life. Select a vocation which helps realize your ideal compassion.

12. Do not kill. Do not let others kill. Find whatever means possible to protect life and to prevent war.

13. Possess nothing that should belong to others. Respect the property of others but prevent others from enriching themselves from human suffering or the suffering of other beings.

14. Do not mistreat your body. Learn to handle it with respect. Do not look on your body as only an instrument. Preserve vital energies (sexual, breath, spirit) for the realization of the Way. Sexual expression should not happen without love and commitment. In sexual relationships be aware of future suffering that may be caused. To preserve the happiness of others, respect the rights and commitments of others. Be fully aware of the responsibility of bringing new lives into the world. Meditate on the world into which you are bringing new beings.

After developing these 14 precepts, Nhat Hanh added this personal comment: "Do not believe that I feel that I follow each and every of these precepts perfectly. I know I fail in many ways. None of us can fully fulfill any of these. However, I must work toward a goal. These are my goals. No words can replace practice, only practice can make the words."

Nhat Hanh has also been refreshingly open to other religions. He has studied Christian texts, particularly the New Testament Gospels, expressing deep appreciation for the teachings of Christ. In fact, he has written several books showing common connections between his Buddhist faith and Christianity: *Living Buddha, Living Christ* and *Going Home: Jesus and Buddha as Brothers* have been well received by Christian readers.

Nhat Hanh's appreciation for the wisdom found in all religious traditions was evident in a 1999 encounter where he had been invited to visit prisoners at the Maryland Correctional Institution at Hagerstown. During a question-and-answer period, an incarcerated man asked: "I have a Christian background. Is it okay if I practice meditation?" Hanh answered, reflecting his great respect for all religious traditions: "I think it is possible to profit from many traditions at one time. If you love oranges, you are welcome to eat them, but nothing prevents you from enjoying kiwis or mangoes as well. Why commit yourself to only one kind of fruit when the whole spiritual heritage of humankind is available to you? It is possible to have Buddhist roots as well as Christian or Jewish roots. We grow very strong that way."

Because he values all religious movements, Nhat Hanh does not seek converts. In fact, just the opposite is the case. Speaking with a reporter from the *Jerusalem Post*, he said: "Everywhere I go I urge people to stick to their roots. You remain a Jew when you practice the teaching I offer and you become, maybe, a better Jew (or a Christian or a Hindu). You have to help make your tradition grow in the direction that will help the young people go back to it because I know that a person who gets uprooted from his tradition is an unhappy person."

After a 38-year exile, Nhat Hanh was permitted in 2005 to visit Vietnam. Though he had been banned for decades, his books were consistently smuggled into Vietnam and reproduced. As a result, he was very well-known, respected and loved even though most Vietnamese had never seen nor met their teacher. *Time* magazine described the moment of return: "It was a homecoming more fitting for royalty or a rock star than a monk. The 1,000 or more devotees who waited in the chilly dawn at Hanoi's Noi Bai Airport clutched bouquets of flowers, sang songs, and jostled for a better view. For a bunch of Buddhists, they were pushy. When Thich Nhat Hanh finally stepped out of immigration, they surged forward with a force that crushed people against doors and tore sandals, hats and gloves off dozens of others. 'I touched him! I touched him!' shouted one woman, who then burst into tears."

Reflection: Wisdom from Thich Nhat Hanh

If in our daily life we can smile, if we can be peaceful and happy, not only we, but everyone will profit from it. This is the most basic kind of peace work

There is no enlightenment outside of daily life.

People deal too much with the negative, with what is wrong. Why not try and see positive things, to just touch those things and make them bloom?

When you have compassion, you can touch compassion everywhere. When you have violence and hatred, you will connect with those energies around you. This is why it is very important to select the channel you want to be on.

In order to rally people, governments need enemies. They want us to be afraid, to hate, so we will rally behind them. And if they do not have a real enemy, they will invent one in order to mobilize us.

The miracle is not to walk on water. The miracle is to walk on the green earth, dwelling deeply in the present moment and feeling truly alive.

In every cell of your body you can find both heaven and hell. The higher or lower spiritual force is right there.

Action: How to Be like Thich Nhat Hanh

1. Push back the darkness. When a village was bombed, Nhat Hanh's followers were dispatched to rebuild it. Then it was bombed two more times and rebuilt twice more. People were ready to give up hope because with each rebuilding, the village was bombed. Yet, Nhat Hanh gave instructions to rebuild. "What is the point of rebuilding a village when you know it will be bombed again?" he was asked. Nhat Hanh told them if they did not rebuild the village it would mean they had given in to despair.

2. View everyone as a potential Buddha, even those who may be hostile toward you. When Nhat Hanh was finally allowed to visit Vietnam he knew he would be observed and followed by police. "We don't mind because we believe police officers also have the Buddha nature. If you radiate joy, compassion, understanding, peace and calm, they will be able to appreciate it and profit from it," he told a reporter.

3. No matter what activity you are engaged in, perform it with awareness and joy. At Plum Village, the community established by Nhat Hanh, there is a carved wooden sign beside the walking meditation path which summarizes moment-by-moment awareness and joy: "The mind can go in a thousand directions, but on this beautiful path, I walk in peace. With each step, the wind blows. With each step, a flower blooms."

4. When others become fear driven and angry, rekindle their compassion. On September 11, 2001, during the terrorist attacks on New York City, Nhat Hanh was in the United States. As many Americans were demanding retribution and revenge, Nhat Hanh spoke with a magazine writer saying: "We must wake up to the reality of our situation. Compassion is the only means for our protection."

5. Become an anger specialist. "As practitioners, we have to be anger specialists," Nhat Hanh reminds followers. "We have to attend to our anger; we have to practice until we understand the roots of our anger and how it works. Accept your anger because you know, you understand, that you can take care of it; you can transform it into positive energy."

6. **Routinely take time to count your blessings.** Nhat Hanh often tells people to take a pen and sheet of paper. Sit at a desk, or better still, go into nature and sit at the base of a tree. There compile a list of all the things that make you happy right now— clouds in the sky, flowers in the garden, children playing, two eyes in good condition, etc. Putting together a gratitude list becomes an effective reminder that we all have enough to be happy now. And when we feel happy, fear and anger are displaced.

7. **Remember that you can meditate anywhere, anytime.** When people ask Nhat Hanh, "How do I find time for meditation when I'm so busy?" his answer is astonishingly simple: "You can practice walking meditation between meetings, on the way to your car, up or down the stairs." Whenever he needs to be at an airport, he arrives much earlier than is necessary "so I can practice walking meditation there. Friends want to keep me until the last minute, but I resist. I tell them that I need the time."

8. **Spend time in the presence of deeply spiritual people.** "When we see such persons, we feel peace, love and strength in them and also in ourselves," Nhat Hanh says. "When a sage is present and you sit near him or her, you feel peace and light." Take advantage of opportunities in your community to hear and be present when sages visit.

9. **Learn about another religion.** If you're Christian, study another faith in-depth and make friends with someone who is of the faith you are researching. In addition, visit your friend's place of worship. Nhat Hanh spent considerable time studying the Christian Gospels. He also cultivated many Christian friendships. Both of these helped him appreciate the teachings of Christ.

10. **Find someone to love.** "Do you have someone to love?" Nhat Hanh asks in his book *Teachings on Love.* "We all want to love and be loved. If you do not have anyone to love, your heart may dry up. Love brings happiness to ourselves and to the ones we love." If you're married or in a relationship, love your partner deeply. If you're single, find someone to love and love that person profoundly and without reservations.

Books by Thich Nhat Hanh

Living Buddha; Living Christ.
The Long Road to Joy: A Guide to Walking Meditation.
The Miracle of Mindfulness.

3

Ben Salmon

Catholic Conscientious Objector of the "Great War"

There is no such animal as a "just war." —Ben Salmon

A letter dated June 5, 1917, was addressed to President Woodrow Wilson by a young man who had recently registered with his local draft board. Though he had complied with the newly created Selective Service Act, he wrote the President saying: "Complying with your edict, I registered today. Your mandate was autocratic, and contrary to the Constitution ... I refuse to submit to conscription. Regardless of nationality, all men are my brothers. God is 'our Father who art in heaven.' The commandment 'Thou shalt not kill' is unconditional and inexorable.... Both by precept and example, the lowly Nazarene taught us the doctrine of non-resistance, and so convinced was he of the soundness of that doctrine that he sealed his belief with death on the cross."

For his convictions, this young man was arrested, given a military court martial, sentenced to death—a sentence which was commuted to 25 years of hard labor in prison.

The letter writer was Ben Salmon, a pacifist who refused to accept alternative or noncombatant service in the military. Though there were a handful of others who refused military service—mainly from historic peace churches such as Mennonite, Quaker, and Seventh Day Adventist—Salmon stood out from all of them because he based his pacifism on his Roman Catholic faith.

Born in 1899 to a working class Catholic family in Denver, Ben Salmon had attended Catholic schools. In the early 1900s there were a series of labor struggles across the nation which made him sensitive to social-justice issues. Thus in his 20s, Ben became a union activist, picketing and protesting for better working conditions. He helped organize the Railway Clerks' Union in Denver, an action which caused him to be dismissed from his job on the Colorado and Southern Railroad. In 1916 he campaigned strongly for Woodrow Wilson because he was the "non-intervention" candidate opposing America's entry into the European war.

Thus, he and many other Americans were stunned when Wilson reversed himself declaring that the United States needed to enter the war "to make the world safe for democracy." On April 2, 1917, Wilson asked and received from Congress a declaration of war on Germany. Initially it was hoped that volunteers would meet the need for soldiers. However, due to lower than expected enlistments, Wilson requested Congress to pass a Selective Service Act for World War I requiring all males aged 21 to 30 to register with their local draft boards. This was in effect from May 18, 1917, through December 20, 1918, during which time more than 24 million American men registered.

The war and mandatory selective service created a crisis of conscience for Salmon. Brought up by devout Catholic parents who took their children regularly to Mass, Salmon absorbed a deep faith and the values the church taught him—kindness, compassion, love for God and neighbor. In his letter to President Wilson, Salmon wrote: "I am not an alien sympathizer. I was born in Denver, of Canadian-American parents, and I love America. This letter is not written in a contumelious spirit. But, when human law conflicts with divine law, my duty is clear. Conscience, my infallible guide, impels me to tell you that prison, death, or both, are infinitely preferable to joining any branch of the army, and contributing, either directly or indirectly to the death of my fellow workingmen."

This could not have been an easy decision to make. He was 28 and had been newly wedded to Elizabeth Smith, a local Denver woman from a prominent family. Her father, Samuel Charles Smith, was a highly visible Denver citizen, the owner of many restaurants and food stands around the city. Salmon's letter launched a bitter struggle between a solitary young Catholic man and the government of the United States. Though Salmon applied for conscientious objector status, something the U.S. government made provision for among historic peace churches, Roman Catholics were not included because the church taught and adhered to a "just war" theology.

Though Salmon knew that laws about draft resistance were severe and harsh he nevertheless wrote his local draft board clearly stating his position: "I am legitimately entitled to an exemption: a wife and mother to support. However, I will not use my dependents to shield me from an institution against which my soul rebels." His letter concluded: "Let those that believe in wholesale violation of the commandment 'Thou shalt not kill' make a profession of their faith by joining the army of war. I am in the army of peace, and in this army I intend to live and die."

The response was swift. On January 5, 1918, he was arrested and released on $2,500 bond. Adjusted for inflation, that would have been nearly $50,000 today. Another man out on bail would probably have reconsidered his position. Would he continue to resist any and all military service or could he accept noncombatant duty such as a medic, cook, clerk? In Salmon's case there was no need for further thought. His convictions were firm as made clear the following day when he published an article in a small weekly paper which he distributed to family, friends and parishioners at St. Catherine of Sienna Church in Denver. Titled "Killing the Wrong Men" he stressed the commandment "Thou shalt not kill," applying it even to war. "But, if killing has to be insisted upon, those responsible for wars—kings, presidents, kaisers, etc.—should be made to fight each other and not drag millions of innocent youths into a game where they would be compelled to slaughter each other."

Salmon's letter and interviews with the draft board were quickly making him Denver's most vocal opponent of the war.

His position was not shared by the vast majority. His own beloved Knights of Columbus, upon reading his January fifth letter, voted to expel him from the organization. Though hurt by the action of fellow Catholics, Salmon continued to stress the importance of the Catholic church in his life. He wrote: "It must be understood that the action of the Knights of Columbus did not in any way affect my affiliation with the Catholic church, except of course that it prejudiced many Catholics against me."

On March 30th, Salmon went on trial defended by two Denver attorneys. Found guilty, he was sentenced to nine months in the Denver County Jail, but appealed his case and was again released on $2,500 bond. Meanwhile, whatever defense he could claim was weakened considerably by an order issued on April 27, 1918, by War Secretary Newton D. Baker who directed action against all conscientious objectors "whose attitude ... is sullen and defiant," "whose sincerity is in question," or "who are engaged in propaganda." The order mandated that such individuals were subject to military trial and conviction by court-martial.

Three weeks later Salmon received notification from the draft board that he had been inducted into the Army. He protested reminding the draft board there was a rule which prohibited induction of any person out on bail in a criminal process. The draft board acknowledged his induction was "irregular" but that he had to comply. Salmon decided he would refuse to report for duty.

This resulted in his prompt arrest and being turned over to the military where he was placed in solitary confinement at Fort Logan, Colorado. He was ordered to serve in any capacity, but again refused indicating any involvement, even that of a noncombatant, was aiding the war effort. Writers at the *Denver Post*, in an article that week, went after Salmon with a vengeance describing him as "the slacker, pacifist, the man with a yellow streak down his spine as broad as a country highway ... who loved the German flag more than the Stars and Stripes." The article included descriptions of Salmon as "pro-German" and "anti-American," adding he was "the man who laughs when brave Americans are dying on the battlefields of France."

After repeated attempts to coerce and pressure Salmon into service, the military decided to he would be tried in military court for "desertion" and "propaganda". He was found guilty and initially sentenced to death, which was then commuted to 25 years in prison. Salmon was incarcerated in Leavenworth and other federal penitentiaries spending weeks at a time in solitary confinement. At one point he spent six months in "the hole"—a medieval-type dungeon located directly over the prison sewer system, a windowless, humid, vermin-infested cell measuring five feet by nine feet and containing no bed or blanket.

Though he was unfairly and often harshly treated by his captors, Salmon never wavered from his pacifist stance. There was, however, one painful issue which created the temptation to lash out violently which revolved around the unfortunate death of his brother. Joe Salmon was not just a younger brother to Ben, but his closest friend. In December 1918, Joe took a leave of absence from his employment in Bakersfield, California to visit his brother at Christmas. He arrived at Leavenworth in Kansas on December 14th where he was detained at the prison gate and questioned at length. He was finally allowed to visit with Ben for half an hour. Ben had just been placed in "the hole" the previous day. Joe promised to return for a second visit on Christmas Eve. After visiting with cousins in Chicago, Joe made his way back to Kansas in a snowstorm. Because of a streetcar operators' strike, he had to walk several miles through a blizzard to reach the prison. There he spent several hours trying to gain admittance, but was turned down. Finally Joe gave up, deciding to go to Denver to visit his mother. On that trip he came down with pneumonia and died within days after Christmas.

Upon learning of his brother's death several weeks later, Ben was broken with grief. Because Joe had not yet been given a funeral, Ben asked Colonel Rice, the prison commandant, for a compassion leave to attend the service in Denver. The request was denied without explanation. Ben's grief turned to rage at Rice blaming him for Joe's death because he was not permitted to enter the prison during the snowstorm. Ben candidly wrote about his feelings: "I felt for a while as if the strain would drive me to do violence to the man whom I considered mainly responsible, viz: Colonel Rice, the commandant of the prison. I studied the matter over thoroughly, and afterwards thanked God once again for religion, for if unrestrained by religious impulses, nothing could have kept me from seeking an opportunity and murdering Colonel Rice, so acute was my reaction to his merciless attitude."

While incarcerated, Salmon also had to contend with his own church's support of the militarism via the "just war" theology. He staked out his position not merely on political and humanitarian grounds, but upon his Christian-Catholic religious grounds. Salmon's pacifism put him at odds with his own church. For example, Cardinal John Farley of New York remarked in 1918 that "criticism of the government irritates me. I consider it little short of treason.... Every citizen of this nation, no matter what his private opinion or his political leanings, should support the President and his advisers to the limit of his ability."

Farley along with the majority of Catholic bishops supported Wilson citing the "just war" teaching of the church. Salmon, however, objected to this teaching hand writing a 200-page manuscript critiquing the church's "just war" theology. His only reference tools were a Bible and *The Catholic Encyclopedia*. This was a remarkable achievement for a man whose education ended with the eighth grade. In that manuscript, Salmon declared: "If you are a Christian, listen to the voice of Christ echoed from the pages of the New Testament." He cited Christ's blessing of the "peacemakers" (Mt 5:9) and the "merciful" (Mt 5:7) and noted that Jesus said, "Do not murder" (Mt 19:18). In Salmon's Catholic ethic there was no such thing as a "just war."

After two years of prison, Salmon announced he was beginning an indefinite hunger strike to protest his treatment. In a letter written to the Secretary of War as well as the military commandant of Fort Douglas where he was incarcerated, Salmon said: "For more than two years I have been illegally imprisoned because I refused to kill or help kill. I will not kill.... I wish to inform you that I am on a hunger strike for liberty or death ... because I am opposed to militarism—wholesale murder—you have tortured me in diverse ways for 26 months, and you now have me in the prison guard house, an unhealthful abode of solitude where one keenly feels the want of fresh air and sunshine. I have missed my meals for four days, and I will continue to starve until released by a discharge from prison or by death."

After two weeks, authorities began to force feed Salmon. Though this kept up for several months, Salmon continued to lose strength becoming weaker and weaker. Charging that he was mentally ill, authorities transferred him to St. Elizabeth's Hospital for the Insane in Washington, DC. Finally, fearful that he would die, and not wanting publicity, Salmon was released from prison in 1920. Also, by then, several attorneys, including members of the American Civil Liberties Union, had taken an interest in his case.

Salmon returned to his wife and family, moving to Chicago where he lived a quiet life. Incarceration, however, took a toll on his health contributing to his early death, at age 43, on February 15, 1932. To the end, he remained a faithful, devout Catholic. Of his three children, one became a priest, another a Maryknoll Sister.

Reflection: Wisdom from Ben Salmon

If Christians would have the same faith in their God that non-Christians have in a mere materialistic idea, "Thy Kingdom come" would shortly be a reality in this world of sorrow and travail.

Love, of course, is like everything else, relative. Christ did not expect me to love a stranger as much as I love my mother. But even though love is relative, it never reaches a level so low as to warrant an injury.

Non-resistance does not mean to say nothing or do nothing ... non-resistance means, not a cowardly, submissive attitude, but a courageous, aggressive use of our intellect and a Christian exercise of the good spirit within us.

The opposite of love is hate, and the amount of hate that finds expression in every war ... warrants the conclusion that war is hate and peace is love.

The trouble with us is, we are afraid that Christ's rule of life will not work ... We are actually afraid to practice his teachings for fear that we might lose out in the experiment.

The successful way to overcome the evil of war is by the good of peace, a steadfast refusal to "render evil for evil."

Action: How to Be like Ben Salmon

1. Pray for your enemies. Salmon was horribly mistreated by prison officials and even other prisoners, yet, in a letter to prison officials he said: "I pray to God to give you light to see the Truth, and grace to follow it. May He forgive you for past offenses!"

2. Don't accept a "no" answer as a final one. As forces in the Denver area lined up against Salmon, he began to see support come from outside his community. His initial contact with the American Civil Liberties Union was disappointing. He asked them for their help and endorsement as a conscientious object. Their reply: "Supreme Court has held conscription constitutional. No use fighting. Writing." Salmon refused to take their "no" as a final answer and kept fighting. Later the ACLU came to his assistance.

3. Do what you can with what you have. Salmon's education ended at the eighth grade yet while in prison he hand-wrote a sophisticated 200-page manuscript critiquing the church's "just war" theology.

4. Remind yourself that people can change their attitudes toward you. Two years after the Denver Knights of Columbus expelled him from their organization, Salmon received a letter from John B. McGuaran of the Denver Knights expressing regret over their treatment. McGuaran told Salmon: "Most of the member thought you were dealt with in an unjust manner." When people oppose you, try to remind yourself they can change their minds as they see your resolve.

5. Let people change and allow their changing attitudes to soften your heart. When Salmon received that letter from McGuaran, it not only encouraged him but tempered his cynicism about support from fellow Catholics. He did not allow his resentment to grow larger.

6. When your cause is just, people become supportive. Though Salmon was misunderstood and even resented by many, gradually people came to admire his courageous convictions. One woman wrote: "I know that the same magnificent courage that has sustained you through will continue to sustain you ... for strong spiritual forces are working on your side."

7. Never become bitter over experiences. In site of all he suffered, Salmon was remembered as an entertaining host and a loving father. He did not allow his spirit to be infected with bitterness.

8. Be guided by your conscience. Catholic army chaplains tried to dissuade Salmon from his position citing the "just war" theology taught by the church. Salmon respectfully disagreed citing from the teachings of Christ and deferring to his conscience not their authority. "A mistaken, though well-meaning, clergy cannot dissuade me from the course, he wrote.

9. Try to retain a sense of humor. As serious as his circumstances were, Salmon continued to exhibit a sense of humor. When he was placed in St. Elizabeth's Hospital for the Insane, he described his fellow patients this way: "The wilder ones rave and holler, all day long they rant and screech ... only when they become exhausted do they consent to use a little judgment. Oh, it is delightful!"

10. Keep the faith. No matter what issues tumble into your life, keep the faith. Though his church was never at the forefront of support, Salmon remained faithful to the end of his life, attending Mass regularly. During Holy Week, he would fast on Good Friday, Holy Saturday and Easter Sunday.

Book about Ben Salmon

Unsung Hero of The Great War by Torin R. T. Finney

4

Bede Griffiths

Christian Guru

It is no longer a question of a Christian going about to convert others to the faith, but of each one being ready to listen to the other and so to grow together in mutual understanding. —Bede Griffiths

Beginning in the 1970s and continuing on through the next decades, people from all corners of the world made a long, tedious journey to Trichy, a city in south India. Once there, they made their way to Shantivanam, a Christian Ashram headed by a British Roman Catholic Benedictine monk who looked more like a *sannyasin,* an Indian holy man. At times, so many came that the ashram facilities were swamped with guests even sleeping on the outdoor balconies.

One man who made the journey was a New York City cab driver. After listening to and meeting with the holy man, the cab driver expressed the experience of many saying: "Leaving him you felt transformed—your whole inner state was changed because of his atmosphere of peace and spiritual power. I always felt changed when I left him after a private talk."

The individual so many traveled to be with in India was Father Bede Griffiths also known as Swami Dayananda. During his lifetime he emerged as one of the outstanding spiritual leaders, sages and mystics of the 20th century. Almost single-handedly, he ushered in a new era of inter-religious spirituality.

Born near London in 1906, he was named Alan Bede Griffiths, the fourth child of a middle-class Anglican family. He received a scholarship to Oxford University where he studied literature and philosophy from 1925 to 1929.

Upon graduation, Griffiths and two companions—Hugh Waterman and Martin Skinner—pooled resources and purchased a country cottage in rural Eastington. Their plan was to live in utter simplicity, supporting themselves mainly by milking a few cows and selling the milk to villagers. During the one year they lived that way, the three read, studied and discussed the Bible. This broadened the flickering flame of spirituality already inherent in Griffiths' life. Impressed by the moral and ethical principles of Christianity, Griffiths felt he needed to take the next step in his spiritual evolution, but was uncertain what that step should be. Over the next year, he continued his own reading and study of the Gospels.

In turn, that led him to consider Christian theology and history so he read the *Summa Theologica* of St. Thomas Aquinas, concluding it provided "the complete philosophical justification for Christianity." He also read thoroughly the *Ecclesiastical History of the English People* by Bede, the monk known for his scholarly study of English history and whose name Griffiths would late adopt. Now, Griffiths knew what his next step would be: to explore entry into the Roman Catholic church. This was not an easy decision for him, as his family for generations were Church of England (Anglican).

Griffiths sought out and met with a parish priest, Father Palmer, who provided him with additional readings and spiritual conversation. On Christmas Eve, 1931, Griffiths was received into the Catholic church and received his first communion at midnight Mass.

The next year Father Palmer took Griffiths to visit a nearby monastery, the Prinknash Priory, a community of 30 Benedictine monks. For Griffiths it was literally love at first sight. He'd found a spiritual home and was deeply moved by the order and dignity of monastic life, as well as the kindness and compassion he experienced from the monks. He decided to become a monk and on January 15, 1933, was clothed as a novice taking the name Bede. In 1937, he took final vows as monk and proceeded studying to become an ordained priest. His ordination to the priesthood took place on March 9, 1940, though Griffiths continued to live and work as a monk.

The year 1954 became pivotal for Griffiths for he met Father Benedict Alapatt, an Indian Benedictine who wanted to minister in India. Father Benedict asked Griffiths if he would join him in that task. The timing of that request was providential because Griffiths had secretly been exploring his expanding interest in Eastern religions. Father Benedict's invitation excited him greatly. Griffiths wrote to a friend saying he was off to India "to discover the other half of my soul."

His curiosity about Eastern spirituality was not academic but personal and reflected his early disillusionment with aspects of Christianity. Writing to a friend, he explained: "I had begun to find that there was something lacking not only in the Western world but in the Western church. We were living from one half of our soul, from the conscious, rational level and we needed to discover the other half, the unconscious, intuitive dimension. I wanted to experience in my life the marriage of those two dimensions of human existence, the rational and intuitive, the conscious and unconscious, the masculine and feminine. I wanted to find the way to the marriage of East and West."

In March, 1955, Griffiths, now nearly 50, set out for the three-week journey from the Port of London, via the Straits of Gibraltar, Suez Canal and on to Bombay (Mumbai), India. Upon arrival in India, Griffiths lived initially in a Western-oriented Benedictine monastery near Bangalore (South India). However, he felt the familiar Gregorian chants, monks' habits and daily routine bore no relationship to life in India, so he left.

Griffiths next stop was the Kurisumala Ashram in the mountains of Kerala. There he felt free to begin the experiment of developing connections between Hindu and Christian, Indian and Western spiritualities. He began to dress as an Indian *sannyasa*,

Eleven Mystics

wearing orange robes, going barefoot, sitting and sleeping on mats, eating simple meals of rice, curry, vegetables and pineapples (no meat, fish, eggs, cheese, bread, jam or pudding)—eating all from plain earthenware dishes purchased locally. From 1955 until 1968 Griffiths' work at Kurisumala was satisfying and successful. The ashram became increasingly self-supporting, attracting adherents from the community and abroad.

In 1968 Griffiths was asked to take over the Shantivanam (Forest of Peace) Ashram near Trichy, in south India. The founder, a French monk had died of cancer and the ashram needed a new leader. The arrival of Griffiths inaugurated a transformation of the ashram. Under his leadership, it became a center for inter-religious dialogue and spiritual contemplation.

Griffiths himself modeled the approach. For example, he embraced meditation as a spiritual practice, something more common to Hindu gurus than Christian clergy. Though his meditation followed the Hindu pattern of using a mantra as the focus, his mantra was the Jesus Prayer—"Lord Jesus Christ, Son of the Living God, have mercy on me, a sinner." In a letter to his friend Nigel Bruce, Griffiths responded to his questions about his meditation practice. Griffiths response provides a clear glimpse of his daily meditation practice:

> To answer your questions:
>
> 1) My meditation period is normally an hour in the morning & an hour in the evening, but it is sometimes shortened slightly (3/4 hour) sometimes lengthened to 2 or 3 hours, but not commonly.
>
> 2) I find that the words of the Jesus Prayer normally repeat themselves. Sometimes it seems to gather strength & one prays in a concentrated manner.
>
> 3) Sometimes the words "fade out", but rarely completely so. They seem to go on "in the heart". One may not notice them, but one finds them going on, as it were.
>
> 4) If thoughts really intervene and cut off the prayer, then I renew the mantra again—or it renews itself, as soon as I realize what has happened.
>
> 5) Yes, I regard the concentration on the person of Jesus as

*very important. I feel that it puts one in touch with the concrete
reality of his person, & "focuses" the mind. To me this is the
difference between Christian & Buddhist & Hindu prayer. Christian prayer reaches the Center in & through Christ.*

Gradually, Griffiths' fresh approach at integrating the wisdom
and spirituality of two faiths, Christian and Hindu, began to attract more and more people. For many, Griffiths became their
Christian guru and they came from all over the world to sit under
his teachings and be in his presence. He personally made the Shantivanam Ashram world famous. Those who came experienced from
him both a compassion and an openness which they found refreshing and liberating. In his presence people found themselves ener-
gized for new spiritual growth and evolution. And this happened
because Griffiths himself was never stagnant, but ever evolving
spiritually.

For example, in the 1930s Griffiths was more limited in his
view. Commenting upon these words ascribed to Jesus—"I am the
way and the truth and the life. No one comes to the father except
through me" (Jn 14:6)—Griffiths acknowledged that other religions
contained truth but felt "there is only one absolutely true religion
... Christ is the Way, the Truth and the Life, without him no man
comes to the Father." However in the 1970s he felt that Biblical
passage needed clarification and wrote: "Christ is the ultimate
fulfillment, the final and definitive word of God, but the same
cannot be said of Christianity. Christianity, as an organized religion seeking to express the mystery of Christ, the divine Word, in
human terms, suffers from the same defects as other religions."

There was yet a third evolution in Griffiths' thought. As he
read, studied other religions, prayed and meditated, Griffiths came
to the conclusion that all religions are complementary, expressing
a single, same Truth. In his 1976 book, *Return to the Center,* he
wrote: "Saivism, Vaishnavism and Shaktism, and the different
schools of Vedanta in Hinduism, Hinayana and Mahayana Buddhism, with their different schools, the Sunni and Shia sects in
Islam, and their different schools of philosophy, Catholicism, Or-
thodoxy and Protestantism within Christianity, with their differ-

ent expressions of the one Truth of revelation, each with its particular insight. But one must learn to discern among these conflicting and partial views the principle which unites them, which transcends these differences and reconciles their conflicts."

As his spirituality evolved and matured, he became alarmed by the rigid traditionalism of the church and asked: "Could not the church be more aware of the tremendous search for God, for a new consciousness beyond the mental consciousness, for a new age of spirituality which many believe is now dawning? The Christian experience of God is unfathomable depth, but it is locked up in words and formulas, which have for many lost their meaning."

Though Griffiths was well received by many, there were criticisms. One came from the local bishop who objected to Griffiths' "Indianization" of Catholic rituals and teachings. Griffiths adopted the garb and outward appearance of an Indian *sannyasin*, going barefoot with long hair and beard and clothed in a shawl with a length of orange-colored cotton knotted at the waist. When Griffiths celebrated daily Mass he followed the established Roman Catholic rite, but with the addition of familiar Hindu gestures and symbols. Community prayers consisted of Psalms, Bible readings and Catholic hymns, but were always preceded by a Sanskrit chant and a reading from Hindu sacred texts.

Upon learning of these practices, the bishop insisted that Mass not be celebrated sitting on the floor, that an appropriate altar be used, and that Griffiths wear "normal" attire and not the traditional Hindu robes. Griffiths, however, did not change his ways, pointing out that the Shantivanam ashram was independent and not subject to diocesan control. Interestingly, Griffiths was left untouched by officials in Rome, probably because he did not hold a teaching position in a seminary or Catholic university. Others believed it was his personal holiness and sanctity which provided him with a buffer from Roman ecclesiastical discipline. Griffiths, however, was convinced it was geographical distance which spared him, saying that India was a long way from Rome.

More fierce criticism came from some Hindu spiritual leaders. One swami, taking a swipe at Griffiths, wrote: "As these priests know our rites and traditions and are aware of our sensibilities, by what right or authority do they wear the ochre robe?... Bede Griffiths has no grasp at all of the Indian psyche ... he is meddling with the soul of a very old and sophisticated people by continuing his experiments at Shantivanam."

The swami went on to call Griffiths a "spiritual colonialist" adding: "You abuse and pervert our symbols and traditions to your own motivated missionary ends.... You have not transcended religion and you have no intention of doing so, whatever your pious declarations. You have an overriding ambition to subvert and subsume us with our own spiritual concepts."

Griffiths defended himself pointing out that other Hindus—Vivekananda, Gandhi, Ramakrishna and others—remained firmly Hindu while appreciating there was truth in Christianity as well. Griffiths reminded the swami he considered himself Christian in religion, but Hindu in spirit.

In addition he noted that outward signs and rituals were human creations designed to tap into a greater reality: "All religious teachings are a symbolic expression of a truth which cannot adequately be expressed. Each religion, be it Christian, Hindu, Buddhist, Muslim or whatever, is limited by time, space and circumstances. All forms of organization, priesthood, ritual and doctrine belong to the world of signs which will pass away. But in all these superficial forms of religion, an eternal truth manifests itself. Idolatry consists of remaining in the realm of these signs; true religion goes beyond the sign to reality."

While Griffiths' conviction that there is an underlying unity among all the great religions made some uncomfortable and uneasy, his message of love and unity resonated with a great many more. Through his own example, people could see the possibilities for a deeper spiritual and mystical life by remaining open and welcoming to insights from other religious traditions. Though rooted in his own Christian, Catholic tradition, he bore witness to a Truth he believed was the object of spiritual searching.

Well into his eighth decade, Griffiths suffered two serious strokes. The first in December 1992, the second in January 1993.

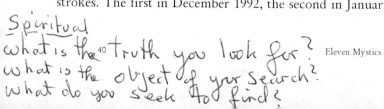

Spiritual
what is the ⁴⁰ truth you look for?
what is the object of your search?
what do you seek to find?

Eleven Mystics

He recovered only partially and died peacefully on May 13, 1993. The following day Bishop Gabriel of Tiruchirapalli presided over a memorial service saying: *Dom Bede Griffiths is a great gift to the Indian church. He is a saint.*

Reflection: Wisdom from Bede Griffiths

I suddenly saw that all the time it was not I who had been seeking God, but God who was seeking me. I had made myself the center of my own existence and had my back turned to God.

God has graced every tradition with insight into the divine mystery, from the most primitive to the most sophisticated—each has a gift to bring to the world.

The CAll FOR THOSE WHO know IS TO —

The call of the church today is to transcend the limits of the institutional structures and to open itself to the presence of the Spirit in the church and in every Christian. + in every human Being in the World

EVERYWHERE —? For God Made them

God had brought me to my knees and made me acknowledge my own nothingness, and out of that knowledge I was reborn. I was no longer the center of my life and therefore could see God in everything.

SPIRIT

The concept of one world, one human race and one religion based on the Universal Wisdom has acquired a new significance, as a way to escape from the disastrous conflicts which are dividing the world today.

All religious teachings are a symbolic expression of a truth which cannot adequately be expressed.

Action: How to Be like Bede Griffiths

1. Focus on what unites people rather than what divides. Be open to truth in other religions. Try not to harbor a negative, condescending attitude toward people of other faiths; rather, remain open to them, their experiences, their worship, their scriptures.

2. Don't give in to discouragement. Life does not always run smoothly. This was true for Griffiths who wrote a friend: "The life at the ashram here is not going too well and I sometimes wonder whether I can cope with it. I don't seem able to keep people together and enable them to live in peace." Nevertheless, Griffiths continued on and things began to change for the better.

3. Read widely. Griffiths was a lifelong reader, devouring books on a wide variety of subjects. If you're accustomed to reading on spirituality from your own tradition, broaden your reading experience. Pick up books by writers from different traditions. Doing this will deepen your own faith.

4. See God in nature. Early in his life, Griffiths noted: "What I am discovering is the intimate relation between nature and God. God is present in nature, in every created thing..." See God when you're walking through a forest, while gardening, when looking at a flower or tree.

5. Consider simplifying your life. Griffiths lived the life of a simple monk. He traveled light, going long distances with nothing other than a spare robe, a towel, some soap, a comb and a few books. His meals were simple and without meat. You don't have to become as ascetic as Griffiths did, but his life challenges us to search where we can simplify.

6. Meditate. This was an important spiritual practice for Griffiths and the source of his inner peace and outer joy. If you don't know how to meditate, join a meditation group or buy some books and learn some techniques.

7. Practice hospitality. Though Griffiths was busy writing, teaching and lecturing, he was always hospitable to others. He answered letters by hand from people seeking advice. When visitors arrived at the ashram, the first person they saw was his tall figure standing at the gate to greet them personally. Every day he handed out the ashram mail himself, mainly to remain in regular touch with ashram guests.

8. Respond when you see someone in need. When visitors came to the ashram and were obviously wounded emotionally or spiritually, Griffiths would often invite them to come to his hut in the evening and sit in quiet meditation with him.

9. Listen to people. Griffiths was a magnet for others, not

Eleven Mystics

only because of his spirituality, but because he listened carefully and compassionately. He seldom gave advice or offered direction. Rather, he followed the conversation with an understanding heart. In his presence, people opened up and spoke freely, honestly. Do this for the people in your social circle.

10. Be patient. Griffiths spent a lonely and frustrating two years at Shantivanam with a constantly changing group before a small but loyal community formed around him. There is very little overnight success in any endeavor. Patience and perseverance are prerequisites for success.

Books by Bede Griffiths

The Marriage of East and West
The Golden String

5

Abraham Heschel

Militant Mystic

For many of us, the march from Selma to Montgomery was about protest and prayer. Legs are not lips and walking is not kneeling. And yet our legs uttered songs. Even without words, our march was worship. I felt my legs were praying.
—Heschel's letter to Martin Luther King, Jr., 1965.

In March, 1965 when Martin Luther King, Jr. planned the historic march from Selma to Montgomery, Alabama, he was joined by several religious leaders. One of those was Rabbi Abraham Heschel who walked with King leading the column of civil rights demonstrators as they slowly marched through the streets of Selma. They were surrounded by hostile crowds who shouted obscenities and displayed banners expressing both racism and anti-Semitism—"Koons, Kikes and Niggers Go Home!" was the message on one sign.

After the march was over, Heschel and some companions went to the Montgomery airport arriving both tense and hungry. Stopping at a snack bar to buy a meal, Heschel faced yet more hostility. The woman behind the counter expressed her disapproval of Heschel and his companions. Looking directly at the white bearded Heschel she spoke sarcastically: "Well, I'll be damned. My mother always told me there was a Santa Claus, and I didn't believe her, until now."

Heschel smiled at her and asked to buy food. She said there was none available. Continuing to smile, Heschel spoke softly and

Eleven Mystics

gently: "Is it possible that in the kitchen there might be some water?" The woman said there was. "Is it possible that in the refrigerator you might find a couple of eggs?" Again she said yes. "Well, if you take the eggs and boil them in the water, that would be just fine," Heschel said. The woman frowned at him: "And why should I?"

"Why should you? Well, after all, I did you a favor."

"What favor did you ever to do me?"

"I proved there was a Santa Claus."

The woman burst into laughter. A tense standoff was relieved and the woman began to prepare meals for Heschel and his companion. Heschel managed to offset hostility by humor.

That incident, reported by Edward K. Kaplan in his book *Spiritual Radical: Abraham Joshua Heschel in America*, reveals the two sides of Heschel's personality: prophetic in his action against racial injustice and pastoral in his response to a hostile woman. Through Heschel's life one sees clearly how the spiritual should impact the social.

Abraham Joshua Heschel was born into a family whose members could count back seven generations to prominent Hasidic rabbis. In fact, his ancestors founded and expanded the Hasidic movement, a Jewish mystical group started in the 18th century. Born in Warsaw, Poland, in 1907, Heschel was groomed to follow in the lineage of Hasidic leaders. Resisting family pressure, he chose to pursue a secular education, studying philosophy in Warsaw and later at the University of Berlin which awarded him a doctorate in 1933. In Berlin, Heschel also took Judaic courses at a nearby Orthodox theological school and became part of a tiny minority of young Jewish scholars who fit seamlessly into both the secular world and the small circle of Orthodox Judaism.

He began teaching in Berlin as the Nazis were increasing in popularity and power. By 1938 they were strong enough to begin expelling Jews from Germany. That year Heschel was arrested by the Gestapo and deported back to Poland. A few months before Germany invaded Poland, Heschel was able to emigrate via the assistance of Julian Morganstern, president of Hebrew Union College in Cincinnati, who had been feverishly working to obtain visas for European Jewish scholars.

Though Heschel escaped, the remainder of his family—mother and three sisters—all died at the hands of the Nazis (his father had died in 1917). Though he would travel worldwide, Heschel never returned to Germany, Austria or Poland saying: "If I should go to Poland or Germany, every stone, every tree would remind me of contempt, hatred, murder, of children killed, of mothers burned alive, of human beings asphyxiated."

From 1940 until 1945, Heschel taught at Hebrew Union College, but those five years were very difficult for him. He was without any family, his English was weak, and the college was associated with Reform Judaism. The student body, faculty and administrators adhered to a liberal form of Judaism and expressed little appreciation for his Orthodox diet and Hasidic spirituality. They were also years of grieving for him: the loss of his family, the loss of his country, the loss of his work as a professor in Berlin, the destruction of Jews all over Europe. His bereavement was punctuated only by his becoming a naturalized U.S. citizen in 1945 and meeting concert pianist Sylvia Straus, whom he married in December, 1946.

Earlier that year, Heschel was invited to join the faculty of New York's Jewish Theological Seminary (JTS)—which he gladly accepted, becoming its first professor of Jewish ethics and mysticism. By then, Heschel had mastered English and was also fluent in Polish, Yiddish, Hebrew and German.

Though he would emerge to become the major Jewish thinker of his generation, the faculty at JTS were not necessarily appreciative nor supportive of Heschel. "As Heschel gained stature outside the seminary, his alienation from most of his colleagues increased," writes Kaplan. Because he was a practical theologian rather than a speculative one, "he was never accepted as a peer by the faculty," says Kaplan. "Even in the JTS chapel, Heschel did not fit in. At the 7 a.m. morning service, he was the first to arrive; wrapped in his tallith and tefillin, he paced around as he prayed, swaying back and forth, eyes tightly closed in ardent concentration. The other professors sat stiffly, dignified and did not move when they prayed."

Although Heschel's main tasks were that as a professor and author, he was not a hopeless idealist. There was a practical, earthiness about him, evidenced during a period when he served on the admissions committee of the seminary. At the time, students wishing to attend JTS were required to be interviewed by this committee. During one interview, Heschel remained quiet as other professors asked questions of the student. Finally, he turned to the candidate asking: "If you were going to Alaska, what two things would you take with you?" Wanting to provide the "right" Jewish answer, the potential rabbinical candidate said, "I would take tallith and tefillin,"—the Jewish shawl and two leather boxes used for morning prayers. Professor Heschel looked at the student asking: "Wouldn't you take a warm coat?"

The year 1962 was pivotal in Heschel's life. His book, *The Prophets*, was published and was well received. That publication also coincided with his emergence as a modern prophetic voice for social justice which was grounded in a profound spirituality of life. He became friends with Martin Luther King, Jr. and in 1965 risked his life marching from Selma to Montgomery. His daughter, Susannah Heschel, a professor at Dartmouth College, recalls conversations in their home about the role of nonviolence, the power of religious faith and theology to combat racism. "You cannot worship God," he would say "and then look at a human being, created by God in God's own image, as if he or she were an animal."

She remembers feeling concerned, even frightened when her father left home to march with Rev. King. "I was a child in 1965, but I remember vividly when my father left our home in New York City to take part in the Selma March. He was a Jewish theologian who had long been active with Dr. King, lecturing and writing on behalf of the Civil Rights movement.... When my father went to Selma, we were all nervous. John Lewis ... had tried two weeks earlier to lead a march across the Pettus Bridge and the Alabama state troopers had rioted against the demonstrators, beating Lewis and others severely.... I vividly recall when my father left home two weeks later for Selma, kissing him good-bye, watching him get into a taxi to go to the airport and wondering if I would ever see him again. The next few days were tense, and when my father returned from the march, I was relieved and proud."

Heschel's desire to join with Martin Luther King, Jr. was not a political act, but a spiritual one. His daughter explains: "For my father, the march was not simply a political demonstration, but a religious occasion. He saw it as a revival of prophetic Judaism's political activism and also of the traditions of Hasidism, a Jewish pietistic revival movement.... He said it reminded him of the message of the prophets, whose primary concern was social injustice, and of his Hasidic forebears, for whom compassion for the suffering of other people defined a religious person."

It's clear Dr. King welcomed, appreciated and respected Heschel's strong and visible support. He described the rabbi as "one of the great men of our age, a truly great prophet." Dr. King added: "He has been with us in many struggles. I remember marching from Selma to Montgomery, how he stood at my side. I remember very well when we were in Chicago for the Conference on Religion and Race.... To a great extent his speech inspired clergymen of all faiths to do something they had not done before."

After King's assassination, Heschel said: "Martin Luther King is a sign that God has not forsaken the United States of America. God sent him to us ... his mission is sacred.... I call upon every Jew to hearken to his voice, to share his vision, to follow in his way. The whole future of American will depend upon the influence of Dr. King."

Like King, Heschel went on to oppose the Vietnam War, again emphasizing that for him it was not political, but spiritual and moral. At an anti-war rally he proclaimed: "This is not a political demonstration. It is a moral convocation, a display of concern for human rights." Citing Leviticus 19:16—"Neither shalt thou stand against the blood of thy neighbor, I am the Lord"—he said public opposition to the Vietnam War was a religious obligation, "a supreme commandment."

Another injustice Heschel addressed was the attitude of Christians toward Jews. He began confronting this issue by establishing a warm relationship with Cardinal Augustin Bea who was designated by Pope John XXIII to review Catholic theology about Judaism. Cardinal Bea asked the American Jewish Committee to prepare talking points on issues they would like to explore.

Heschel was part of the Jewish team preparing documents for the Vatican and it was his memorandum, "On Improving Catholic-Jewish Relations," which was presented to the Vatican. The two main points stressed in the 13-page document were: a) that the church condemn anti-Semitism, rejecting once and for all the charge that the Jewish people as a whole are responsible for the crucifixion and death of Jesus; and b) that the church renounce the teaching of contempt for Judaism, acknowledging the value of Jews as Jews.

In 1965 when the Vatican released its statement, *The Relation of the Church to Non-Christian Religions,* it contained a softer, gentler, positive approach to Judaism saying "God holds the Jew most dear" and that "the Jews should not be presented as rejected or accursed by God." The Vatican statement also criticized anti-Semitism stating the church "decries hatred, persecutions, displays of anti-Semitism, directed against Jews at any time and by anyone."

While Heschel despaired over anti-Semitism, especially as it evolved into the horror of the Holocaust, his faith in God and humanity remained firm. In an essay titled "Abraham Heschel: A Memoir," Rabbi Arthur Green explains: "It was too easy, Heschel felt, to blame God for the Holocaust. The failure, he insisted, was essentially a human one. It was the depravity of human beings acting in defiance of faith that had given us the concentration camps. It was human beings, transgressing what he insisted was religion's most essential teaching, the creation of every person in God's image, who had brought about the unimaginable degradation of their fellow humans.... Our task, Heschel insisted, was not that of reconstructing religions but of rebuilding humanity. If humanity had failed, the only thing to do was to be more human and to show others how to be more human. This could be done only by example, and example is what Heschel provided."

Because of tensions and conflicts among the Jewish, Christian and Muslim religions, Heschel was once asked "Would it be a better world if we were all of one religion?" Responding in the traditional rabbinic fashion of answering a question with a question, Heschel said: "If I were to ask the question whether the Metropolitan Museum should try to introduce the policy that all the paintings should look alike, or I should suggest that all human faces should look alike, how would you respond to my proposal?"

Though Heschel did not enjoy affirmation and appreciation of his Jewish academic colleagues, his writings and life impacted people and politics, theology and ethics far beyond the boundaries of his Orthodox Jewish faith. Protestants, Catholics and an entire generation of Jews were inspired and influenced by Heschel.

One accolade which came his way was the appointment (1965) as a visiting professor at Union Theological Seminary in New York City, the leading Protestant school of theology at that time —and he was the first Jewish appointee at that venerable institution. In fact, his influence over Christians was so strong that some called him "apostle to the Gentiles." Abraham Joshua Heschel died from a heart attack in his sleep at home in 1972. A few months later, *America*, a prominent Catholic magazine, devoted an entire issue to his life and thought. Reporting on his death, *Time* magazine described him as the "militant mystic."

Reflection: Wisdom from Abraham Heschel

Wonder, rather than doubt, is the root of knowledge.

Morally speaking, there is no limit to the concern one must feel for the suffering of human beings, that indifference to evil is worse than evil itself, that in a free society, some are guilty, but all are responsible.

In Biblical days prophets were astir while the world was asleep; today the world is astir while church and synagogue are busy with trivialities.

A religious man is a person who holds God and man in one thought at one time, at all times, who suffers harm done to others, whose greatest passion is compassion, whose greatest strength is love and defiance of despair.

We teach children how to measure, how to weigh. We fail to teach them how to revere, how to sense wonder and awe.

God is of no importance unless he is of supreme importance.

America has been enticed by her own might. There is nothing so vile as the arrogance of the military mind. Of all the plagues with which the world is cursed, of every ill, militarism is the worst: the assumption that war is an answer to human problems.

We are not asked to abandon life and to say farewell to this world, but to keep the spark within aflame, and to suffer his light to reflect in our face.

Man is on the verge of spiritual insanity. He does not know who he is. Having lost a sense for what he is, he fails to grasp the meaning of his fellow-man.

Action: How to Be like Abraham Heschel

1. Appreciate every day and live in the present moment. Don't take life, in all of its simplicity and complexity, for granted. Heschel reminded people: "Just to be is a blessing. Just to live is holy."

2. Respond promptly and compassionately when a friend is hurting. Rabbi Jack Reimer tells of being with Heschel when they were informed there was a death in the family of a mutual friend. Heschel insisted he and Reimer leave immediately to visit the grieving family. "We went to the airport, we flew to Boston, got into a cab, and went to the house. Heschel walked in, he hugged the mourners, he sat silent for an hour. He didn't mumble a single cliché, 'How old was she?' What difference does that make? ... 'I know how you feel.' You don't know how I feel. None of the clichés. He just sat there in silence for an hour. And then he got up, hugged them, and we left. I learned that you don't have to be glib. You just have to care," said Reimer.

3. Find a passionate purpose to your life. It is important not only to have convictions, but also to have the courage of your convictions. Consider Heschel's observation: "According to Albert Camus, 'There is only one really serious philosophical problem: and that is suicide.' May I differ and suggest that there is only one really serious problem—and that is martyrdom. Is there anything worth dying for?"

4. Let scripture study become personally transformative. There are many who study the Bible but not as many who put into practice the biblical principles of love, compassion and social justice. Heschel's moral and ethical actions are derived from the Bible. Let your study of scripture lead you into an engaged spirituality.

5. Allow the Divine to permeate all of life. Heschel believed God is constantly present, but is also constantly blocked by people and institutions. "God will return to us when we shall be willing to let Him in—into our banks and factories, into our congress and clubs, into our courts and investigating committees, into our homes and theaters."

6. Admire the right people. It's too easy to be influenced and swayed by people who are powerful, wealthy or famous. Let your role models be people of compassion. Heschel once admitted: "When I was young, I admired clever people. Now that I am old, I admire kind people."

7. Expand your religious comfort zones. Heschel befriended individuals beyond his Jewish circle. Though he was a conservative and Orthodox Jew, his friends included Protestants, Catholics and liberal Jews. Add to your circle of friends, those of different spiritual traditions.

8. Allow your spiritual awareness to impact social issues. Heschel's spirituality informed his piety, turning it into political action. He was an early critic of the Vietnam War saying: "To speak about God and remain silent on Vietnam is blasphemous." Via Heschel, remember that spirituality and social concern are two sides of the same coin.

9. Don't be neutral: resist evil and injustice. Heschel said the opposite of good is not evil. It is indifference. Take a stand where there is injustice.

10. Express gratitude in all things. Several years before his death, Heschel had a major heart attack. When he regained consciousness, he told a friend: "My first feelings were not of despair or anger. I felt only gratitude to God for my life, for every moment I had lived."

Books by Abraham Heschel

God In Search of Man
The Prophets
Man Is Not Alone

6

Oscar Romero

"Voice of the Voiceless"

I have frequently been threatened with death. As a Christian, I do not believe in death without resurrection. If they kill me, I will be resurrected in the Salvadoran people. —Oscar Romero two weeks before his assassination

In late 1979, Archbishop Romero was visiting an urban slum—a sizeable neighborhood of poverty where entire families lived in shelters made from cardboard, tin and whatever other discarded building materials they could salvage. June Carolyn Erlick, a reporter traveling with Romero that day, asked him: "How do you feel when you see a community like this?" His response was memorable: "I just think of what I have always preached. There should not be first-class people and second-class people."

Oscar Arnulfo Romero, the conservative cleric who became a passionate prophet, was born on May 11, 1919 and a year later baptized into the Catholic church. As a youth he often spent time at the town's two churches during his free time, showing an unusual interest in spirituality and religious life. His family enrolled him in the local public school which ended at the third grade. After that he was privately tutored until he was 13. His father, Santos, then made arrangements for Oscar to apprentice in carpentry, a trade for which he exhibited exceptional talent. He was convinced his son should learn a trade because in El Salvador academic studies seldom led to employment. But due to his interest in spirituality, Oscar was enrolled in the minor seminary at San Miguel when he was 13, followed by the national seminary in San Salvador. He complete his theological studies at the Gregorian University in Rome where he was ordained a priest in 1942. He stayed on in Rome to pursue a doctorate in theology, but his studies were cut short when he was called home to El Salvador in 1944—there was a shortage of priests and he was desperately needed.

His first appointment as pastor was to a rural parish, but his innate gifts combined with his international experience were recognized by church authorities. Soon he was appointed executive secretary of the Episcopal Council for Central America and Panama, then as editor of the archdiocese newspaper, then as chaplain of the church of San Francisco. In 1970 he was made an auxiliary bishop for the archdiocese of San Salvador.

Four years later, Romero was named bishop of Santiago de Maria in Usultan. His three years as bishop coincided with an escalation of government violence against the rural poor. At that time 14 Salvadoran families controlled more than 60 percent of the arable land. The injustice of this inequity of land ownership was not only frustrating for the poor but it kept them in poverty.

Whenever there was an attempt to challenge this status quo, violence was inflicted on those who raised the issue. Romero, aware of the killings, did not speak out publicly, only privately, naïvely believing the killings were aberrant, that they were not government policy, that they would cease when authorities were informed about them. However, Romero was a pastor at heart who visited with and listened to the poor. Little by little and one by one, these impoverished, violated people helped their bishop understand the day-to-day reality which was their world. Important seeds were planted in Romero's mind and spirit, ones which would bear fruit three years later.

In 1977 Romero was appointed archbishop of San Salvador—an appointment met with delight by the government and the military who saw him as a hesitant, timid, conservative cleric. Priests, however, reacted with dismay, disappointment and even despair by his appointment. Romero succeeded Luis Chavez y Gonzalez who had been the archbishop of San Salvador for 38 years. Both moderate and tolerant, Chavez did not prohibit his clergy from supporting the poor and backing peasant rights to organize and challenge landowners and the government. The clergy had hoped Arturo Rivera y Damas, an auxiliary bishop, would follow Chavez. In Rome, however, the decision was made to appoint Romero.

Francisco Estrada's account reveals the deep disappointment in this appointment: "We knew that Rome had been in consultation with various groups since late 1976 in the search for a new archbishop, knowing that Chavez had reached the age of retirement. The nuncio [Rome's official representative to El Salvador] proposed Romero as a candidate and consulted with the government, the military, the business sector and the ladies of society. They asked the rich and the rich gave their complete backing to Romero's appointment. They felt he was 'one of theirs'."

Yet three weeks later an event took place which utterly and profoundly transformed Romero into a courageous, confident and passionate priest, propelling him to become the prophet of El Salvador, speaking in support of the oppressed while challenging the wealthy and chastising the government. He became a surprise in history. The event which turned him upside down was the assassination of a Jesuit priest and personal friend, Rutilio Grande. At that time, the military's efforts at suppressing the people was supplemented by mercenary death squads who freely roamed the country, raping, torturing and killing without fear of arrest. They even were paid a bounty for every person they victimized.

That day Father Grande, a Jesuit whose ministry was among the poor, was traveling the road from Aguilares to El Paisnal. A death squad was waiting and opened fire, killing not only the priest but also Manuel Solorzano, an older man, and Nelson Rutilio Lemus, a teenager. The two were giving Father Grande a ride to the rural church where he was scheduled to celebrate Mass.

Upon learning of the killings, Romero rushed to the parish house in El Paisnal where the three bodies had been carried. There, he celebrated a Mass. Deeply saddened by these deaths, Romero was also equally deeply moved by hearing local sugar cane workers speak highly of Father Grande's ministry among them. Two days later, Romero led a Mass at San Salvador Cathedral which was celebrated by 100 priests before an immense crowd inside and outside the cathedral.

The readings for the funeral were personally selected by Romero. One was from the Gospel of John: "Greater love has no one than this, that he lay down his life for his friends" (Jn 15:13). The other was from an apostolic exhortation of Pope Paul VI who declared: "The church cannot be absent from the struggle for liberation." Referring to Grande and his two companions as "co-workers in Christian liberation," Romero, in this public forum, chastised his country's leaders saying: "The government should not consider a priest who takes a stand for social justice as a politician, or a subversive element, when he is fulfilling his mission in the politics of the common good."

Following the funeral, Romero felt the church he led needed to respond to the murders. It was an agonizing decision, but Romero took three steps. First, he wrote the president of El Salvador, Colonel Molina, informing him that, as archbishop, he was "not willing to participate in any official act of the government as long as the latter did not put all its effort into making justice manifest in regard to this unprecedented sacrilege." Second, Romero informed the colonel that the church had published the excommunication of "the authors of the crime."

The third decision was momentous. To show his solidarity and protest the murder of Grande and his companions, Romero made the decision to cancel all Masses throughout the entire country the following Sunday, except for one on the steps of the cathedral. This amounted to a general strike by the church against the government and military. The decision was not made easily nor did Romero make it alone. He convened with all the priests of the archdiocese as well as some women religious. The matter was discussed at length and a vote taken: 71 voted in favor, one against, one abstained. Rome's representative, the nuncio, objected and scolded Romero saying he was "irresponsible" and "imprudent".

Nevertheless Romero proceeded canceling all masses except the one on the cathedral steps to which the people were invited. The response had to be gratifying for more than 100,000 filled the plaza in front of the church. Romero spoke: "I want to give a public thanks today, here in front of the archdiocese, for the unified support that is being expressed for the Gospel and for these our beloved priests. Many of them are in danger, and like Father Grande, they are risking even the maximum sacrifice.... Whoever touches one of my priests is touching me. And they will have to deal with me!" At the mention of Rutilio Grande, the crowd broke out in thunderous applause.

From that point on Romero increasingly became the "voice of the voiceless," using the moral authority of his position as archbishop to speak out on behalf of those who could not do so for themselves—the tortured, the imprisoned, the terrorized masses. In a sermon he declared: "The church is concerned about those who cannot speak, those who suffer, those who are tortured, those who are silenced. This is not getting involved in politics.... Let this be clear: when the church preaches social justice, equality and the dignity of people, defending those who suffer and those who are assaulted, this is not subversion, this is not Marxism, this is the authentic teaching of the church."

Support of the poor became a major spiritual principal for Romero. In a pastoral letter titled "The Church and Popular Political Organizations," he wrote: "It is the role of the church to gather into itself all that is human in the people's cause and struggle, above all in the cause of the poor. The church identifies with the poor when they demand their legitimate rights. In our country the right they are demanding is hardly more than the right to survive, to escape from misery." In his sermons, Romero told those who were violated that he and the church felt their pain: "We suffer with those who have disappeared, those who have had to flee their homes, and those who have been tortured."

In spite of Romero's public support of the people, the government escalated violence against the people. More priests and religious women were killed. Countless numbers of people were arrested, detained, tortured, raped and murdered. Bodies clogged rivers and streams. Tortured and disfigured bodies were left in garbage dumps or simply on the streets of the capital weekly. It is estimated the civilian death toll began to exceed 3,000 per month with some 75,000 to 80,000 Salvadorans slaughtered. More than 300,000 simply disappeared without a trace and millions became homeless fugitives fleeing military and police. All of this within a country whose population was 5.5 million.

As opposition was silenced, Romero was left alone speaking out against the atrocities and in support of the people. Even Romero's sermons changed. Rather than simply study Biblical texts and expound on them, Romero tied scripture to currents events as they unfolded. To prepare for his weekly homily, Romero did two things: first, he met for several hours with a team of priests and lay people to discuss and reflect on the situation in the country that week, listening carefully. The second was prayer.

An eye witness to Romero's style of weekly sermon preparation recalls: "The meeting [with advisers] would end, he'd say good-bye to the group, then he'd sit down to organize his ideas and prepare himself. I'm a witness, having seen him on more than one occasion in his room, on his knees, from ten on Saturday night to four in the morning on Sunday, preparing his homily. He would sleep a little while and then be at the cathedral by eight."

Romero was so comfortable with what he would say in church that he stepped into the pulpit with nothing more than a slip of paper with two or three ideas written on it. In his sermons, Romero not only tried to support the victimized but boldly spoke to those committing the violence asking them to reconsider, repent and be converted.

In one homily he said: "And so, brothers and sisters, I repeat what I have said here so often, addressing by radio those who perhaps have caused so many injustices and acts of violence, those who have brought tears to so many homes, those who have stained themselves with the blood of so many murders, those who have hands soiled with tortures, those who have calloused their consciences, who are unmoved to see under their boots a person abased, suffering, perhaps ready to die. To all of them I say: No matter your crimes. They are ugly and horrible ... but God calls you and forgives you."

Another time he addressed soldiers and police officers directly, pleading with them to cease the violence: "I would like to appeal in a special way to the men of the army, and in particular to the troops of the national guard, the police and the garrisons. Brothers, you belong to our own people. You kill your own brother peasants; and in the face of an order to kill that is given by a man, the law of God should prevail that says: 'Do not kill!' No soldier is obliged to obey an order counter to the law of God. No one has to comply with an immoral law.... Therefore, in the name of God, and in the name of this long-suffering people whose laments rise to heaven every day more tumultuous, I beseech you, I beg you, I command you in the name of God: 'Stop the repression!'"

The moral and spiritual leadership was provided by Romero alone, without the support of his fellow bishops, leaving him feeling lonely. He had hoped for support from his peers, yet they all turned against him, except for one. A small group of bishops went so far as to file official complaints about him to the nuncio, sending a secret ten-page letter directly to the pope, charging Romero's pastoral approach was Marxist, that he was unduly influenced by radical priests and that he enjoyed the popularity he received from the people for his criticisms of the government. Romero learned of the letter and was pained by it, yet his diary entry reveals his resolve in spite of being isolated by fellow bishops:

"They [the bishops] denounce me to the Holy See in matters of faith, say I am politicized, accuse me of promoting a pastoral work with erroneous theological grounds—a whole series of accusations that completely impugn my ministry as a bishop. In spite of how serious this is, I feel a great peace. I acknowledge my deficiencies before God, but I believe that I have worked with goodwill and that I am not guilty of the serious things of which they accuse me. God will have the last word on this."

On March 24th, Romero was celebrating Mass at a small hospital chapel when he was shot and killed. It is widely believed the assassins were members of notorious Salvadoran death squads. This view was later supported by an official UN report which identified several former El Salvadoran military leaders as involved in the assassination. The news of his assassination sent shock waves across the country and around the world. Some 250,000 came to pay their respects. As a large crowd, numbering in the tens of thousands, gathered in the square outside the cathedral in honor of Romero, a series of small bombs were thrown into the crowd. Simultaneously, there were rapid volleys of gunfire shot at the people from different directions. The attack critically injured hundreds and killed nearly 50. As gunfire and chaos continued, Romero's body was buried in a crypt beneath the sanctuary.

With the death of Romero, the many tensions existing in El Salvador exploded. The country erupted into a horrific civil war which lasted twelve years causing 75,000 deaths. Though bullets silenced Romero, his life has not been forgotten. He is considered by many as the unofficial patron saint of the Americas. His name has been brought forward for sainthood. Even outside of Catholicism, Romero is honored and respected. He is one of the ten 20th-century martyrs depicted in statues above the great west door of Westminster Abbey, the Church of England cathedral in London.

Interestingly, in an interview only two weeks before his assassination, Romero referenced the many death threats he received saying: "Martyrdom is a great gift from God that I do not believe I have earned. But if God accepts the sacrifice of my life then may my blood be the seed of liberty, and a sign of the hope that will soon become a reality.... A Bishop will die, but the church of God—the people—will never die."

Reflection: Wisdom from Oscar Romero

The mission of Christ—to bring good news to the poor, to those who receive only bad news, to those who feel only the assault of the powerful, to those who see the riches that make others happy pass them by— to these the Lord has come.

We must save not the soul at the hour of death, but the person living in history.

To each one of us Christ is saying, "If you want your life and mission to be fruitful like mine, do like me ... give your life out of love for others."

We learn to see the face of Christ ... that also is the face of a suffering human being, the face of the crucified, the face of the poor, the face of a saint, and the face of every person.

Those who trample the people must be in conflict with the church.

A church that tries to keep itself pure and uncontaminated would not be a church of God's service to people. The authentic church is one that does not mind conversing with prostitutes and publicans and sinners— as Christ did—and with Marxists ... in order to bring them salvation's true message.

The Word of God has a ... human mission: to love our neighbor means to be concerned about their needs, their concrete situation, and like the good Samaritan, to help the poor fallen by the roadside.

Action: How to Be like Oscar Romero

1. Ask for help when you are struggling. Five days before his death, Romero spoke with foreign journalists and asked them to help him and the Salvadoran people: "You are the ones who bring the photographs of our people to the world.... Help them understand our situation.... Don't forget that we are people, and we are dying, fleeing and taking refuge in the mountains."

2. Love your enemies. Though difficult, this is a foundational teaching of Jesus and something Romero put into practice. Referring to his enemies, Romero said: "I bear them a message of love. I don't hate them. I don't want revenge. I wish them no harm. I beg them to be converted."

3. Avoid being neutral where there is injustice. Neutrality only aids the oppressor. Romero knew this and therefore spoke on behalf of those victimized, even though it brought him opposition: "There is conflict with the church because we take the people's side," he said. "I insist that the church is not looking for a fight with the government, and for my part I do not want disputes with the government."

4. Request the prayers of others for yourself. Romero knew his task was a difficult one so he asked "for your prayers that I be faithful to this promise, that I will not abandon my people. Rather, I will run with them all the risks that my ministry demands.

5. Practice humility. At a family dinner, Romero asked those present what they thought he could do to "achieve unity with my dear brother bishops." He added that if they felt he was the "cause of any obstacle to this unity, them I am willing to fix that."

6. Be bold and courageous. "We do not want to be Judases. We do not want to be cowardly apostles. We want to be faithful," Romero said.

7. Move in larger circles. Don't limit your friendships and associations to a small group of people. Enlarge your comfort zone and social circle because that will enlarge the capacity of your heart. Romero's circles included clergy and laity, the wealthy and the impoverished, factory workers and farmers.

8. Don't ignore those who are wounded and suffering in any way. Those very individuals became a source of joy to Romero—"I say it with immense joy, for we have made the effort not to pass by,... not to circle round the one lying wounded in the roadway, but to approach him or her as did the Good Samaritan."

9. Let scripture shape daily life. This approach was formative for Romero. "We not only read the Bible, we analyze it, we celebrate it, we incarnate it in our reality."

10. Watch for signs of God. According to Romero God is present "where the poor begin to really live, where the poor begin to free themselves,... the God of life is there."

Books about Oscar Romero

Oscar Romero and the Communion of the Saints by Scott Wright. *Romero: A Life* by James R. Brockman

7

Etty Hillesum

Concentration Camp Mystic

Those two months behind barbed wire have been the richest two months of my life, in which my highest values were so deeply confirmed I am so grateful to You God, for having made my life so rich. —Etty Hillesum

These are remarkable words because they were written by a young Jewish woman being held by the Germans in a concentration camp. In the midst of inhumane conditions, Etty Hillesum consistently expressed gratitude, joy and love of God. Under the most extreme circumstances, she found reasons to praise the divine for beauty and goodness.

Very little is know about Etty Hillesum's life. She was born in her parents' home in 1914 in Middelburg, the Netherlands. Her father, Dr. Louis Hillesum, was a professor of classical languages. Her mother, Rebecca, emigrated to the Netherlands from Russia. Etty was the only daughter and had two younger brothers. Jaap became a medical doctor and Mischa was a talented pianist. While in university studying law and Slavic languages, Etty was very much a free spirit spending time in liberal circles but not committing to any particular ideology.

Although little is known about her externally, a great deal of information is available about her internal spiritual life. From 1941 through 1942 Etty kept a diary. During this period, while Germany invaded Holland and began rounding up Jews, she engaged in a prolific correspondence with friends. Those letters were collected and saved. In the 1980s, decades after her death at Auschwitz, two books were published under her name—one her diaries, the other her letters from Westerbork.

Westerbork, a refugee camp which held Etty as well as thousands of other Jews, was set up by Dutch authorities in 1939. At this point, European Jews were fleeing the Nazi's presence in Germany, Austria, Czechoslovakia and Poland. Many made their way to Holland, a country long known for accepting and sheltering Jews. Because of the large influx of Jewish families, the government established this refugee camp, but when the Germans invaded Holland on May 10, 1940, they quickly assumed control of Westerbork turning it into a holding facility from which Jews would be transported to Nazi death camps.

Every Tuesday between 1942 and 1944 a cargo train loaded with Jews left Westerbork for concentration camps as part of Hitler's "Final Solution". Westerbork came to be known as "the last stop before Auschwitz" for more than a hundred thousand Dutch Jews. Etty Hillesum stayed in this camp from July 30, 1942, until September 7, 1943, when she and her family were put on the train to Auschwitz. Most of what is known about her life comes from her time in the camp.

Reading her letters and diaries evokes some confusion about her faith orientation. To Christians, she is a saint. To Jews, she is a martyr. That Hillesum strongly identified with the suffering of her people, the Jews, is clear. However, her growing faith is strongly shaped by her reading of the New Testament and St. Augustine. Her letters and diary entries make it clear she belongs to the tradition of Christian mystics across the ages.

By 1942 the Germans began requiring Jews to wear the yellow star, and then systematically rounded them up, confining them to Westerbork. To prevent panic among them, the Germans created a Jewish Council, administered by leaders of the Jewish community, but the Nazis were simply exploiting the Jewish leaders, using them to reduce fear among the general Jewish population. Directed by the Germans, the declared purpose of the council was to decide which Jews were to be sent off for "labor service" in the time of war. Etty was given a position with one of these councils, a job which exempted her from internment at Westerbork. However, a few weeks after her appointment she volunteered to become a social worker inside the camp.

Though Etty entered Westerbork voluntarily and as an aid worker was permitted to enter and exit freely, that soon changed as she, too, became permanently confined. Rather than become despairing and hopeless, Etty remained courageous and joyful. In the introduction to *Etty Hillesum: Letters From Westerbork,* Jan G. Gaarlandt notes: "In Westerbork her soul found its deepest expression: she placed herself unreservedly at the service of her people. She spurned all attempts by her Amsterdam friends to take her to a safe address (on one occasion, by force) during the time she was still permitted to travel; she rejected all offers to help her escape from camp when, after June 1943, she was no longer allowed to leave it. She was determined to share the fate of her fellow Jews, without bravado, but also without despair."

Her desire to remain and be a positive influence is quite remarkable given the fact that Camp Westerbork contained a community living in the fear that they were destined to be placed on one of the weekly transport trains to a concentration death camp. Don Krausz, a survivor of Westerbork, tells of the impact upon hearing one's name called for transport: "Once a week, on a Tuesday morning at eleven o'clock, a train would leave with a thousand Jews, for Auschwitz How did it work? You were woken up at one o'clock in the morning and a barrack leader would come in and he would read out names from a list and he would be listened to in total silence except that as a name was called out, you would hear a cry, you would hear a sob."

Etty herself, describes the bleak moments when the transport train arrived in the camp. "Slowly but surely six o'clock in the morning has arrived. The train is due to depart at eleven, and they are starting to load it with people and luggage. The camp has been cut in two halves since yesterday by the train: a depressing series of bare, unpainted freight cars in the front, and a proper coach for the guards at the back. Some of the cars have paper mattresses on the floor. These are for the sick" (August 24, 1942).

It was in that climate of fear and despair that Etty Hillesum developed internally and externally promoted faith and hope. Even before confinement, but as the Nazi noose was tightening around the Dutch Jewish community, Etty was experiencing spiritual freedom and joy. She wrote these words in her diary entry for June 20, 1942: "This morning I cycled along the Station Quay enjoying the broad sweep of sky ... everywhere signs barring Jews from the paths and the open country. But above the one narrow path still left to us stretches the sky, intact.... The sky within me is as wide as the one stretching above my head. I believe in God and I believe in man and I say so without embarrassment.... I am a happy person and I hold life dear indeed, in this year of Our Lord, 1942, the umpteenth year of the war."

Later, after being permanently imprisoned at Westerbork, she wrote this prayer of gratitude: "You have made me so rich, O God, please let me share out Your beauty with open hands. ... Sometimes when I stand in some corner of the camp, my feet planted on Your earth, my eyes raised towards Your Heaven, tears sometimes run down my face, tears of deep emotion and gratitude. At night, too, when I lie in my bed and rest in You, oh God, tears of gratitude run down my face, that is my prayer."

In spite of the obvious injustices and atrocities being committed by the Germans, Etty had compassion for them and encouraged other Dutch citizens to do the same. "Do not relieve your feelings through hatred, do not seek to be avenged on all German mothers, for they, too, sorrow at this very moment for their slain and murdered sons. Give your sorrow all the space and shelter in yourself that is it due, for if everyone bears his grief honestly and courageously, the sorrow that now fills the world will abate. But if you do not clear a decent shelter for your sorrow, and instead reserve most of the space inside you for hatred and thoughts of revenge—from which new sorrows will be born for others—then sorrow will never cease in this world and will multiply" (diary entry March 22, 1942).

When she learned a friend harbored hatred for the Germans,

she again stressed the importance of love toward enemies. "We have so much work to do on ourselves that we shouldn't even be thinking of hating our so-called enemies. We are hurtful enough to one another as it is." She reminds the friend that there are "bullies and bad characters" among Jews as well as Germans, adding that "no one is really 'bad' deep down." When her friend protested her words saying "that is nothing but Christianity!" Etty responded: "Yes, Christianity, and why ever not?"

Another example of this attitude of compassion is seen in a letter dated December 18, 1942—which was illegally published by the Dutch resistance who asked Etty to write her impressions of Westerbork. In it she not only detailed camp life but added: "I know that those who hate have good reason to do so. But why should we always have to choose the cheapest and easiest way? It has been brought home forcibly to me here how every atom of hatred added to the world makes it an even more inhospitable place. And I also believe, childishly perhaps but stubbornly, that the earth will become more habitable again only through the love that the Jew Paul described to the citizens of Corinth in the thirteenth chapter of his first letter."

In the summer of 1943 the Jewish councils created by the Germans were disbanded and Etty was relieved of her position as a camp social worker, becoming a "camp inmate". Even when she lost the little freedoms she had as a Jewish social worker, Etty's faith, joy and optimism continued to manifest themselves.

In a letter to friends dated July 3, 1943, she tells them: "The misery here is quite terrible; and yet, late at night when the day has slunk away into the depths behind me, I often walk with a spring in my step along the barbed wire. And then time and again, it soars straight from my heart the feeling that life is glorious and magnificent, and that one day we shall be building a whole new world. Against every new outrage and every fresh horror, we shall put up one more piece of love and goodness."

Soon Westerbork became a Nazi concentration camp—crowded, filthy, little food and water carefully rationed. As the horror of life in the camp evolved, Etty was comforted by these words of

Jesus—"Therefore do not worry about tomorrow, for tomorrow will worry about itself. Each day has enough trouble of its own" (Mt 6:34). Calling this "the great lesson from Matthew," she said, "This is the only attitude that allows you to carry on at Westerbork." In fact, Etty drew spiritual strength from the New Testament. As the darkness descended on Holland's Jewish community, Etty records several passages which she read and reflected upon. Her diary entries in September 1942 include these readings:

- *Matthew 6:33—"But seek first his kingdom and his righteousness, and all these things will be given to you as well."*
- *Matthew 5:23—"Therefore, if you are offering your gift at the altar and there remember that your brother has something against you..."*
- *1 Corinthians 13:3—"If I give all I possess to the poor and surrender my body to the flames, but have not love, I gain nothing."*

Etty also found spiritual insight and nourishment in the writings of the Christian theologian Augustine. "I am going to read St. Augustine again. He is so austere and so fervent. And so full of simple devotion in his love letters to God. Truly those are the only love letters one ought to write: love letters to God."

Though Etty may be misunderstood as being young, naïve and idealistic, she was very much aware of the unfolding events and in touch with the harsh reality. One morning as Etty was helping new women arrivals, one of them asked her: "Could you tell me, please, could you tell me, why we Jews have to suffer so much?" Etty later wrote: "I couldn't answer."

In a diary entry, Etty acknowledges: "Of course, it is our complete destruction they want! But let us bear it with grace. There is no hidden poet in me, just a little piece of God that might grow into poetry. And a camp needs a poet, one who experiences life there, even there, as a bard and is able to sing about it."

She was successful in this. Others frequently told Etty she seemed to have nerves of steel while they languished in depression and despair. "I don't think I have nerves of steel, far from it," she wrote in her diary (October 8, 1942), "but I can certainly stand up to this. I am not afraid to look suffering straight in the eyes. And at the end of each day, there was always the feeling: I love people so much. Never any bitterness about what was done to them, but always love for those who knew how to bear so much although nothing had prepared them for such burdens."

As more and more Jewish people were transferred out of Westerbork, time began to run out for Etty and her family. On September 7, 1943, they were placed on a transport train to Poland. Her father, mother, and Mischa boarded Wagon No. 1. Etty was in Wagon No. 12. (Her brother Jaap was transported later).

From the freight car, Etty scribbled this note to her friend Christine van Nooten and threw it out of the train. It was found by farmers and publicly posted by them. Even her final words reflect her vibrant faith and elegant dignity: "Christine, Opening the Bible at random I find this: 'The Lord is my high tower.' I am sitting on my rucksack in the middle of a full freight car. Father, Mother and Mischa are a few cars away. In the end, the departure came without warning. On sudden special orders from the Hague. *We left the camp singing...* " [italics mine].

Their transport reached Auschwitz on September 10, 1943. That same day, her parents were gassed. Mischa died on March 31, 1944. Her other brother Jaap was finally sent to Westerbork at the beginning of 1944. He did not survive the war. The Red Cross reported Etty Hillesum died in Auschwitz on November 30, 1943. She was 29.

Reflection: Wisdom from Etty Hillesum

I do believe it is possible to create, even without ever writing a word or painting a picture, by simply molding one's inner life. And that, too, is a deed.

We have to fight them daily, like fleas, those many small worries about the morrow, for they sap our energies.

Ultimately, we have just one moral duty: to reclaim large areas of peace in ourselves, more and more peace, and to reflect it towards others. The more peace there is in us, the more peace there will be in our troubled world.

The externals are simply so many props; everything we need is within us.

Eleven Mystics

Suffering has always been with us, does it really matter in what form it comes? All that matters is how we bear it and fit it into our lives.

God is not accountable to us for the senseless harm we cause one another. We are accountable to Him!

Whether or not I am a valuable human being will only become clear from my behavior in more arduous circumstances.

We go too far in fearing for our unhappy bodies, while our forgotten spirit shrivels up in some corner.

Action: How to Be like Etty Hillesum

1. See yourself as one who helps others heal. "We should be willing to act as a balm for all wounds," said Etty. In the camp, Etty was one who tended physical wounds, listened to emotional pain and sought to restore broken spirits.

2. Do something! Just because you can't do everything or solve the entire issue, don't hold back. Do whatever you can, however small it may feel. This was Etty's pattern in the horrific conditions of a Nazi prison.

3. Tap into your faith always but especially when times are tough. "My God, apart from You, everything here is quicksand," wrote Etty. The surest and strongest foundation anyone can have is faith and trust in the Divine. "I don't feel I'm in anybody's clutches; I feel safe in God's arms," Etty declared.

4. When you need it, ask. Too many people suffer in silence, going all their lives without some basic needs being met simply because they don't ask. Etty kept corresponding as long as she could. Often she asked if friends could send small items to relieve the misery. "I have one request, if you don't think it too immodest: a pillow or some old cushion; the straw gets a little hard in the end." Etty frequently asked for items needed by others in the camp as well.

5. Smile more often. Be certain to smile at family, friends and even strangers when you see each other. Someone criticized Etty for smiling so much saying, "It's unforgivable to smile at all in times like these." Her response: "I think he's wrong." No matter what the circumstances, Etty offered a warm smile toward the people she encountered.

6. **Don't blame God** when things don't go as planned, when things go completely wrong. Etty wrote a friend advising: "Life is good after all, it's not God's fault that things go awry sometimes, the cause lies in ourselves. And that's what stays with me, even now, even when I'm about to be packed off to Poland with my whole family."

7. **When in need, don't hesitate to ask friends to pray for you.** As Westerbork became more and more crowded, there were times when Etty, in her capacity as a social worker, could not leave, nor did she have a place to sleep. In one letter she wrote a friend saying, "I hope I'll find a bed tonight, every square millimeter is taken. Please pray a little for us."

8. **Strengthen your body when under stress.** In spite of being confined, Etty was determined to exercise by walking in her cell. She calculated that she could take ten steps from one end to the other and chose to "walk" five miles each day in that space. She broke those miles up into seven daily segments: two in the morning, two before lunch, two after lunch, and one before sleeping.

9. **See God or Christ in every human being.** Etty was absolutely certain that life is meaningful and beautiful. That view came out of her desire and ability to see "something of God" in every human being.

10. **Release love on a daily basis.** Etty unleashed her own war against war by releasing love for everyone, agreeing with the Buddha who said: "Hatred does not cease by hatred, only by love."

Books by Etty Hillesum

Etty Hillesum: Letters From Westerbork
An Interrupted Life: The Diaries of Etty Hillesum

8

Caryll Houselander

"Neurotic" Mystic

*The one thing she (Mary) did and does is the one thing that
we all have to do, namely, to bear Christ into the world.*
—Caryll Houselander

In early 1942, an unusual but fascinating medical referral took
place. Dr. Eric Strauss, one of Great Britain's most distinguished
psychiatrists and neurologists, quietly began sending emotionally
disturbed boys to spend time with a woman who was a spiritual
writer, wood carver, poet and mystic. Her name was Caryll
Houselander.

This was a most curious triangle of relationships. First, there
was Dr. Eric Strauss, a distinguished and highly regarded British
medical doctor who would become president of the Psychiatry
Section of the Royal Society of Medicine and of the British Psychological Society. Second was Caryll Houselander with no formal
training in either medicine or psychology. She had come to Dr.
Strauss' attention through her volunteer work at a school for boys
who had been traumatized by the war, many of whom responded
immediately and positively to her sensitive spirit. Third were the
boys sent by Dr. Strauss to Caryll, all of whom were suffering
from what today would be called *Post Traumatic Stress Syndrome*
as a result of the war—one boy, for example, had lived alone in
the Malayan jungle after the murder of his parents.

These boys were sent one by one to Caryll Houselander after

all traditional medical and psychological therapies proved ineffective. Under Caryll's care and her intuitive application of music and art therapy as well as patient listening, the boys quickly recovered from their psychological scars and wounds. As word of her success with traumatized boys spread, other doctors soon began sending their adult patients.

Houselander's biographer Massie Ward interviewed Dr. Strauss asking him about the work Caryll had done for him. Dr. Strauss explained he was so impressed with Caryll's work with the boys that immediately after the war he unhesitatingly sent her adult patients for what he called "social therapy." Intrigued by the phrase, Ward said: "Forgive my dense ignorance, but what exactly is 'social therapy'?" Strauss replied: *With Caryll, it meant she loved them back to life.*

Caryll Houselander (1901—1954) was a living paradox. On the one hand she had a deep and profound spirituality which connected with an amazingly wide spectrum of people. On the other hand she battled with a variety of issues: a chain-smoker, she was painfully shy, at times seriously anorexic, often frail physically. She struggled with issues of abandonment, suffered from panic attacks and covered her face with a chalky white substance giving her a grotesque appearance. Those were some of the reasons she was labeled "neurotic" by her physicians.

In fact, she considered herself damaged goods. One physician, however, was more complimentary saying she was not neurotic, but a highly sensitive individual. Because of her own trials and traumas, she was empathetic to the emotional and psychological wounds of others which allowed her to connect in a deep way with suffering people. Through the 1940s and early 50s, Houselander emerged as one of Great Britain's fascinating mystics and writers on spirituality. She penned 15 books and wrote more than 700 poems, short stories and articles.

Born in Bath, England, Houselander's parents were Willmott and Gertrude Provis Houselander. Caryll was the second of two daughters. Her sister, Ruth, was four years older. The family, while not extremely wealthy, was financially prosperous enough to permit luxuries and had a nurse and governess for the children. Willmott had time to become a skilled huntsman and Gertrude played tennis at Wimbledon.

Their family structure began to change when Caryll was six. At that time Gertrude underwent a strong religious conversion to Catholicism which created distance from her husband who did not share her religious enthusiasm. When Caryll was six, she was baptized into the Roman Catholic church along with her mother.

The impact of her mother's conversion was double-edged for Caryll. On the one side, she found her mother's prayers and practices oppressive. There were long daily prayers, altars set up inside the home and frequent Mass attendance. Caryll referred to her mother's religious orientation as a "persecution of piety." On the other side, however, Caryll was deeply influenced by her mother's devotion and would over time find herself drawn more and more to Catholic spirituality.

Eventually Willmott, who could not accept his wife's religious fervor, left the house and the marriage ended in divorce when Caryll was eight. That event impacted Caryll harshly and it took years before Caryll could properly integrate it into her life. In order to provide for herself and her daughters, Gertrude ran a boarding house. An opportunity emerged for the mother to send Caryll off to a convent boarding school when Caryll was eleven. Thus, in her short life, Caryll experienced parental abandonment twice: once when her father left the house and then when her mother sent her away to a boarding school.

The Convent of the Holy Child school located in a Birmingham suburb was run by French and Belgian nuns. One sister, however, was German and she was the one nun whom Caryll became close to. The sister was intuitively drawn to Caryll, probably because of the little girl's sensitivity and loneliness, and quite probably because the sister herself was a lonely woman as a German working with French sisters just as the First World War was to break out. Animosity between Germans and French was running high. Also, the sister spoke very little English or French and was thus somewhat isolated from the community.

One day as Caryll walked by the room containing convent boots, she saw the German sister alone cleaning a pair of shoes. Caryll went into the room intending to offer her help when she noticed the sister was crying. "Tears were running down her rosy cheeks and falling onto her blue apron and the child's shoes," Caryll would later write in *A Rocking Horse*. Speechless and embarrassed, Caryll did not know what to say or do. They both remained silent for a few moments and then Caryll experienced her first vision.

She described that moment: "At last, with an effort, I raised my head, and than—I saw—the nun was crowned with the crown of thorns. I shall not attempt to explain this. I am simply telling the thing as I saw it. That bowed head was weighed under the crown of thorns. I stood for—I suppose—a few seconds, dumbfounded, and then, finding my tongue, I said to her 'I would not cry, if I was wearing the crown of thorns like you are.' She looked at me as if she were startled, and asked, 'What do you mean?'

"'I don't know,' I said, and at the time, I did not. I sat down beside her, and together we polished the shoes."

When Caryll was 16, her mother abruptly withdrew her from school because she needed her daughter's help running the boarding house. Returning reluctantly, Caryll found herself working for her mother as a domestic servant. One of her many tasks was shopping for groceries and her second vision occurred while she was buying potatoes. At that time in 1918, the major news story was the murder of the Russian czar and the entire royal family. This was much on Caryll's mind.

As she made her way to the potato vendors stall, she was suddenly stopped in her tracks. "I was held still, as if a magnet held my feet to a particular spot in the middle of the road," she recalls. In front of her, as if displayed on a large theater screen, was a "gigantic and living Russian icon." Vividly she saw Christ crucified, his head down, his arms reaching to span the world. Caryll was so moved by her vision that by the time she arrived at the potato vendor's stall, tears were running down her cheeks. The woman selling potatoes, assuming Caryll was in some kind of

Eleven Mystics

trouble, tried to comfort her by giving her an apple after she had purchased the sack of potatoes.

A few days later, she experience part two of the same vision at the same corner. She passed a news stand and saw a newspaper picture of the czar. When she bent down to see the picture more closely, she was startled to see that the face was identical to the face of Christ in her vision. Because of the vision which involved Russia, Caryll soon left her mother's employment and secured a position working with Russian immigrants who had been displaced because of the war and revolution in Russia.

Her third vision which came years later differed considerably from the first two because she saw Christ not in one person such as the German nun or the Russian czar but in all of humanity. That vision took place while she was riding a crowded London subway. "I was in an underground train, a crowded train in which all sorts of people jostled together, sitting and strap-hanging— workers of every description going home at the end of the day. Quite suddenly I saw with my mind, but as vividly as a wonderful picture, Christ in them all. But I saw more than that; not only was Christ in every one of them, living in them, dying in them, rejoic- ing in them sorrowing in them—but because he was in them, and because they were here, the world was here too ... not only the world as it was at that moment, not only all the people in all the countries of the world, but all those people who had lived in the past, and all those yet to come." Caryll said as she emerged on the street from the subway the vision lingered as she saw Christ walk- ing in every pedestrian.

These three visions combined were a source of spiritual en- lightenment for Caryll. Through them she realized that in spite of two world wars, Christians have no enemies; that Christ can be seen in all of humanity. For Caryll the implications of her visions were deep and profound. She would spend the rest of her life see- ing Christ in every person she met. As a result, ordinary life took on a sacramental dimension. She sought to manifest the presence of Christ in her life while seeking to evoke that same presence out of other lives.

When she was 16 and working hard for her mother, Caryll continued to attend Mass. Because of her busy work schedule, it was not easy to find one which fit into her schedule. However she found a church which had a service at noon on Sunday. This meant walking a considerable distance across London to attend that service. Unbeknownst to Caryll, that church continued the practice of pew rental. While there were a few free pews available for visitors, by the time Caryll arrived they were full. Penniless, she slipped into a sixpenny pew.

She recalls what transpired: "I had scarcely knelt down and hidden my face, which was scarlet, when the verger prodded me in the ribs with a collecting bag on the end of a long cane....

"'Sixpence,' said the verger and went on prodding.

"'I haven't got sixpence,' I whispered.

"'All right, then,' said the verger, 'you must go into the free seats.'

"'There isn't one,' I said.

"'Well, then, sixpence.'

"I was scalded. There was a priest standing in the aisle watching the scene. When I sprang to my feet and pushed out of the sixpenny seats, he came forward and put his hand on my shoulder.

"'You're not going, child?' he said. I shook him off.

"'Yes, I am, and I will never come to Mass again.'

"I went, beginning the long walk home again, hardly able to stop my tears of rage."

The angry promise against attending Mass was one which she would keep for eight years before returning. During that time, Caryll did not stop going to church, but began exploring alternative spiritual opportunities. She visited with Anglican priests and attended their services. She attended Methodist church services. During a Salvation Army service she was moved to offer a "testimony", but at the last moment remained silent. Caryll also worshipped in the Russian Orthodox church with some of her Russian refugee friends.

In addition to Christianity, she spoke with representatives of Buddhism and Judaism. After spending considerable time exploring

Eleven Mystics

other religious traditions, she returned to the Catholic Mass, but was a transformed person. During that period of seeking and searching, Caryll made the transition from a faith which previously had been placed upon her by the adults in her life to a faith which was now more clearly defined and based upon her own experience and awareness. Although she came back to the church, she would remain faithful but cautious about faith which was institutionalized.

Caryll and her companions in faith were uneasy about organized Christianity, preferring a more spontaneous and less institutional approach to life. This is evident when they formed a small society to help the poor called "The Loaves and Fishes." In the 1930s when people were feeling the impact of the depression, Caryll had a good position at a company which sold supplies and decorations to churches. Although she was comfortable, Caryll was tormented by the plight of so many who had so little. One day she was speaking with two of the firm's partners, Louis Billaux and Jaxques Doneux, along with several staff members, discussing individuals who were much in need. They identified two problems: how to generate the funds to help and how to provide the help in a way which was not demeaning to the poor.

Their conversation led to a discussion of the Gospel story about Jesus' multiplication of a few loaves and fishes. Abruptly, Caryll said: "Let us put down a penny each. If God wants us to do something, he will multiply it." At that moment, Louis' father, Charles Billaux, walked into the room, looked at the coins laid out on the table. Puzzled, he said, "Whatever those are for, I will multiply them," laying down five shillings. Caryll and her group took that as a divine sign to proceed by forming this small society. That initial group formed the executive committee and each member took turns serving as chairperson. The identity of the chairperson was kept secret. When others joined their efforts, they became known as "Sprats". Those who received help were called "Seahorses". Their ministry grew quickly as each sprat knew of several seahorses in need of aid.

Recipients were usually the poorest of the poor; those who fell between the cracks and were completely ineligible for aid via Britain's welfare system. All assistance was given discreetly so as not to shame or humiliate the recipient. Names of those helped were divulged only when necessity demanded it. The group adhered rigidly to the command of Jesus that giving should be done as anonymously as possible: "When you give to the needy, do not let your left hand know what your right hand is doing, so that your giving may be in secret" (Mt 6:3).

Each sprat tried to catch a "Mackerel"—a wealthy person who would make a donation. Among those helped were those without skills and who could not get work during the depression; the sick and the old who never earned enough to establish any retirement funds; young people who had no family to fall back on for help; refugees. On one occasion, money was given to a woman who suffered from a gum disease causing her to lose her teeth and have bad breath, both of which made it difficult for her to find work. She was given a gift of cash to purchase false teeth. This small, secretive society continued long after Caryll's death.

One aspect of Caryll many found unusual was her odd appearance. When Massie Ward, who with her husband Frank Sheed were cofounders of the publishing firm of Sheed & Ward, decided to write a biography of Caryll, Massie was caught off guard by Caryll's strange looks even though her husband had alerted her. Caryll developed the unusual habit of entirely covering her face with a white, chalklike substance. Ward recalls: "My husband had prepared me for Caryll's appearance. Yet as I stood waiting outside the door of her flat and she came up behind me laden with parcels I was conscious of a genuine shock. The dead-white face, the thick glasses, the fringe of red hair, a touch somehow of the grotesque— it was so surprising as to take one's breath away."

Even Caryll's friends never grew accustomed to her appearance, referring to her makeup as that "abominable chalky-white substance." Many interpretations were offered as to why Caryll covered her face in white. Some thought she was able to hide behind that clown-like whiteness as if she wore a mask. Some thought she didn't want to resemble her mother. Still others

Eleven Mystics

thought she deliberately made herself "ugly" as a form of asceticism to ward off any personal pride in appearance. Interestingly, Ward once asked her why and Caryll replied simply: "I don't like a pink face."

In keeping with some of the biblical prophets who seemed to see and sense things others did not, Caryll was able to see not only with her physical eyes but with her mind. Some might describe her as psychic or one who had the gift of extra sensory perception (ESP). Friends frequently commented that Caryll could "read your mind." To Caryll, this ability was simply a gift from God which was to be used to help others. Before they called on her for help, Caryll was often at their door or visiting at their hospital bedside or calling them on the telephone.

Once Caryll's mother's Siamese cat disappeared. Her mother was fiercely devoted to this small companion and was extremely upset. She phoned Caryll in tears about the animals disappearance. That night Caryll had a dream in which she saw her mother's cat trapped inside a basement cupboard. She immediately phoned her mother. The elder Houselander, who lived in an apartment by herself, at once when down to a disused part of the apartment basement locating a cupboard. Inside the cupboard was her beloved cat.

Because of her books, newspaper columns and published poems, Caryll became inundated with letters from readers. While some wrote to thank her or to compliment her for her wisdom, many wrote asking for advice or seeking encouragement. Caryll answered every letter written to her and this often meant working late into the night and getting less sleep than she needed. In spite of a heavy schedule of working, writing and corresponding, Caryll continued to volunteer her time for the poor and those on the fringes of society. One of the great spiritual experiences of her life took place when she visited patients at a "lunatic asylum" or what today would be referred to as a psychiatric hospital. She records: "I had an incredible day at the lunatic asylum yesterday." Among the patients were several who identified themselves as queens—one of whom permitted Caryll to kiss her hand and who then conferred many titles upon Caryll.

Caryll was especially affected by a simple prayer service held in the small chapel that evening, organized entirely by the patients. She describes the small group which gathered: "An ex-Trappist monk, a young girl, an old lady bent double nearly, but in spite of it and of being insane, beautiful, and a handful of others—all people who had started out in life intent on a high vocation, and now in utter abnegation put away in a lunatic asylum." Yet, that unusual group, facing their own personal issues, reached out in prayer to the world. Caryll was amazed and moved by their prayers, quickly joining them.

When requests for prayer were asked for, she recalls the following petitions: for Russia, for the suffering people of Europe, for the starving people of India, for the sick, for prisoners, for the conversion of the world, for the purity of heart in the world, for pure of heart here. After spending that time in prayer with mental patients, Caryll says her own perspective was greatly clarified: "Think of my grumbling petitions."

In addition to the many demands from readers, Caryll accepted the responsibility of caring for her aging parents as well as an elderly aunt. Once in 1949 a friend expressed disappointment over how little time Caryll spent with her. Caryll replied expressing regret but explaining why her time was so limited: "My father is 80, my mother is 75, and they live in the opposite ends of London. Each has to be visited at least once a week. Then I have an invalid aunt in Brighton, who would like a weekly visit but has to have a two-weekly one or less; there are several neurotic invalids who can't leave their homes, and several people in the mental hospital, also requiring regular and frequent visits. My dinner when alone here only takes about 15 minutes to cook and eat! Also I continue to work while eating it."

That note reveals the depth of Caryll's compassionate caring for others. She was a person who was accessible to those who most needed her and that meant not always being available to friends whose very friendship might have been an important source of nurture for herself.

Caryll's last few years were filled with illness. Beginning in 1949 she suffered from pneumonia, influenza, tuberculosis and finally was diagnosed with cancer. At that time, hospitalization meant being placed in a large public ward, with little or no privacy. Caryll, an introvert, dreaded the thought of being there. The specialist who was to treat Caryll arranged for her to have a somewhat private cubicle at the end of a public ward at Westminster Hospital.

Even in a place which some would characterize as one of humiliation, pain and suffering, Caryll experienced new spiritual growth and awareness. Writing from the hospital to a friend, Caryll explained: "You will be astonished to hear that, much as I dreaded the public ward—and I did dread it, more than the operation—I have now learnt to be glad I am in it, and if I ever come again, which is all too likely, I will choose it!"

Caryll further explained that although she had some privacy inside the cubicle, many of the other patients would come in to visit and their visits were greatly encouraging to her. "My admiration and liking for human nature has gone up by leaps and bounds since I came in there. There is, no doubt, a communion with Christ through pain, which gives people the power of his love, regardless of what, if anything, they believe."

She had surgery, but it left her in great pain and limited hope. In another letter written to a friend, Caryll said: "They say they have removed all the cancer ... but as it was already in the second stage, there is no guarantee at all that it won't return—the chances are about 50—50. After the operation the wound got infected and would not drain properly, and I had a week of real agony, which was helped by drugs, astonishing kindness and wonderful nurses and doctors."

After six grueling weeks in the hospital, she was discharged but had to have daily follow-up treatments of radiation. Caryll knew that her odds of survival were slim. She did not fear death but rather faced that possibility with much calmness of mind and spirit. "I felt no fear of death, though I did not want to die," she said. To another friend she wrote, "I honestly long to be told a hundred percent cure and to return to this life and celebrate it with gramophone records, giggling and gin."

In spite of cancer or perhaps because the cancer threatened to shorten her life, Caryll's appreciation of living deepened. In fact, she experienced some remorse that she did not engage herself more fully with life. "I realized I had never really let myself enjoy life— so many scruples and inhibitions and things preventing me from really enjoying the sheer loveliness of the world, the people in it, and even the material things in it—food, drink, the sun, spending money, etc."

Clearly she was regretting she had lived a life filled with too much austerity. Some of that may have been passed on to her via her mother. "When my poor mother died, in 1950, in St. George's Hospital, I went out into the park opposite the hospital, and sat down and suddenly realized how lovely it was—the sky, the bare trees [it was November], the grass, the very touch of the air—and it suddenly swept over me, with a terrible pang, that my old mother had never really enjoyed life. She was always worried, always working, always thinking about money—never, or certainly hardly ever, sufficiently detached from self to enjoy the beauties and pleasures of this life. Then and there I made up my mind to enjoy my own.... When following hard on this I nearly lost my own life, I made only one resolution: If I was given another chance (as I have been), I would enjoy everything in life that I can, for as long as I can, and as wholly as I can."

Although Caryll soon returned to her normal routines, she was very much aware that her time was short. In the summer of 1954, Caryll's health began to deteriorate. Her physician told her it was unnecessary for her to return for further checkups. At that time, treatment of cancer was limited and the doctor knew there was nothing more which medicine could do for Caryll. She died on October 12, 1954, just a few weeks before her 53rd birthday.

The wonder and lingering impact of Caryll Houselander lies in her eloquent ability to articulate the profound truth that the heart of the Christian faith is love: the love of God and the love of humanity.

Reflection: Wisdom from Caryll Houselander

Love is most likely to spring from another's need for us, and the fact of spending ourselves for another always generates new life in us. To give life is the purpose of love, and we love those people most of all whose needs waken a response in us that floods us with creative energy, causing us to put out new green shoots of life.

Christ is among us. His heart like a rose expanding within us ...

God's will for you is to serve him, in his way, as he chooses now. It is only a want of humility to think of extreme vocations, like being a nun or a nurse, while you try to by-pass your present obvious vocation.... You have to use what you have today, and do not look beyond it.

We go through life with dark forces within us and around us, haunted by the ghosts of repudiated terrors and embarrassments, assailed by devils, but we are also continually guided by invisible hands; our darkness is lit by many little flames, from night-lights to the stars. Those who are afraid to look into their own hearts know nothing of the light that shines in the darkness.

Prayer alone can teach us to concentrate again, can lead us to absolute trust in God, and make our minds ready for other essential things ... for the contemplation (not mere observation) of beauty.

It seems a law of fallen nature that life must always come to its being through darkness, and this makes us even more aware of its beauty. Dawn is lovelier because it comes after night, spring because it follows winter.

To surrender all that we are, as we are, to the spirit of love in order that our lives may bear Christ into the world—that is what we shall be asked.

The beginning of human happiness, and even of human sanity, is to begin to know God. ... Goodness draws the human soul as a tide is drawn by light.

Lift up your eyes and see the star!

The one essential for sanctity is the capacity to love.

Caryll Houselander

The one thing she (Mary) did and does is the one thing that we all have to do, namely, to bear Christ into the world.

Action: How to Be like Caryll Houselander

1. Respond to people's hopes as well as their hurts. Caryll received letters from people who were struggling with depression, chronic illness, divorce (which was judged more harshly in her time) and consequent feelings of guilt. She empathized with their dilemmas and always tried to generate hope. In spite of their life's challenges, she reminded them of God's love for them and of their own innate worthiness.

2. Don't be seduced by materialism. Of course, there's nothing wrong with earning a living or even a very good one. However, don't make the accumulation of wealth your life goal. Caryll had considerable talent as an artist, poet and writer, yet she used her gifts to benefit others rather than just herself.

3. Learn from those less fortunate. One of Caryll's most memorable experiences occurred while she was volunteering at a mental hospital where she had gone to reach out to others and be a blessing to the mentally ill. However, she ended up being helped by the patients and was blessed by her encounter with them. Like Caryll, be willing to learn from others, especially those who occupy a lower place in society.

4. See Christ in every person. In her book, *The Comforting of Christ,* Caryll reminded readers: "If we are not interested in the minds, the feelings, the hopes, the fears, sorrows and joys of everyone with whom we come in contact, we are not interested in Christ. Whatever we do to anyone, we do to him."

5. Help bring out the Christ which dwells within every person. Caryll viewed Mary as a model of the spiritual life saying our task is like that of Mary, namely, to bear Christ into the world. Remember that many people are unaware of the Christ dwelling within them. By both your words and acts, be the one who nurtures and helps give birth to that indwelling Christ.

6. Don't allow your human imperfections to prevent you from making a difference. Caryll had many limitations: she did not have a strong body and suffered from a variety of chronic conditions all of her life. A chain-smoker and so shy some referred to her as a recluse, she even found it difficult to enter a room in her own home when there were other people present. At times she would approach the door two or three times before she finally forced herself to go in. Other times she even failed to persuade herself to enter the room. Caryll suffered frequently from panic attacks, but in spite of such human imperfections, she cultivated and expressed the talents given to her, making a difference to thousands—writing 15 books and penning more than 700 poems.

7. **Be open to sensing the presence of God in the ordinary.** Caryll had three visions, yet, interestingly, those experiences of God's presence took place in very ordinary, daily-life experiences. She had these visions while watching a woman clean shoes, while grocery shopping for potatoes and while glancing at a newspaper at a newsvendor's stand.

8. **Enjoy your life.** Observing her mother, Caryll realized that she had filled her life with too much duty and obligation and not enough leisure and pleasure. Caryll made up her mind to work hard but also to enjoy living. Look at how you live and ask yourself: "Is my life all work and responsibility?" If so, take steps which will bring more beauty and pleasure, spontaneity and play into your existence.

9. **Heighten your sensory awareness.** Much of Caryll's writing shows she drew inspiration from all her senses. She refers to tree bark, delicate blades of grass, the sun's warmth, the sounds of the sea, blight on a green leaf, smells of laundered linens, lemon oil and soap. Recapture the ability to truly see, hear, feel, taste and smell. Be thankful to God for your senses.

10. **Reach out to people marginalized by society.** Throughout her life, Caryll responded to suffering people wherever she found them. She worked with Russian immigrants, refugees, traumatized children, the mentally ill, the poor. When you see a hurt, try to be a healer. Reach out to people who are marginalized by society. Give some of your time to those who can benefit from your wisdom, your experience, your compassionate presence.

Books by Caryll Houselander

The Reed of God.
The Way of the Cross.
Mother of Christ.

9

John XXIII

Mystic Pope

My guiding principles remain the same: humility in every-thing, especially in my speech, union with God and the will of God, and not my own, in all I do. —Pope John XXIII

In the days immediately after being elected pope, John XXIII received a letter from Bruno, a twelve-year-old boy. "My dear Pope: I am undecided. I want to be a policeman or a pope. What do you think?" The new pontiff replied promptly saying: "My little Bruno. If you want my opinion, learn how to be a police-man.... Anybody can be a pope; the proof of this is that I have become one. If you ever should be in Rome, come to see me. I would be glad to talk all of this over with you."

During the tense days of the Cuban missile crisis in 1962, American journalist Norman Cousins acted as an emissary hand-delivering messages between John Kennedy, Nikita Krushchev and Pope John XXIII. As Cousins sat in Pope John's study to report on his encounter with Krushchev, he recalls how the pope, whom he had never met, went out of his way to put Cousins as ease: "'We have very much to talk about,' the pope said. 'Just remember, I am an ordinary man; I have two eyes, a nose—a very large nose— You must feel completely relaxed. We will talk man-to-man.'"

These two stories convey the warmth, kindness and humility which consistently characterized Pope John XXIII, making him one of the most admired and loved popes by both Catholics and non-

Catholics. The man who would become "Good Pope John" was born Angelo Giuseppe Roncalli (November 25, 1881) at a tiny village in the province of Bergamo, Italy. Living under one roof were parents, grandparents, uncles, aunts and their children—28 mouths to feed. All were tenant farmers living in poverty. Angelo Roncalli's humble beginnings are a striking contrast to his predecessor, Eugenio Pacelli (Pope Pius XII), who came from the aristocracy strongly associated with the papacy.

As a child, Angelo lived in an atmosphere of faith instilling in him a deep and profound sense of spirituality. In the household where he lived with his large extended family, the faith was practiced and lived out daily. All children were taught to babble out prayers even before they learned to speak. Each day ended with the entire extended family gathered around a huge kitchen table where the rosary was recited. During the long winter evenings one of the adults read passages of scripture or sections from other spiritual books. On rising daily, the family attended a morning Mass. All of this made an indelible impression upon Angelo. Though most elementary education in the village ended at third grade, Angelo was encouraged to continue his studies.

In 1893, when he was twelve, Angelo took an entrance exam in which he placed third—allowing him entry into a Catholic "seminary" which gave him a high-school education. By the time he was a young teenager, his mind was entirely focused on the spiritual life and service to the church as a priest. At 14 he began to keep a journal which he maintained for the next 67 years. Published as *Journal of a Soul,* it is one of the finest modern spiritual autobiographies available. His first entry begins with a listing of spiritual practices he wanted to engage in. His first priority was to "choose a spiritual director from among the most exemplary, prudent and learned, in whom you may have full trust ... and complete confidence." In the journal he describes what he wanted to do daily, weekly, monthly and yearly. Anyone seeking to evolve spiritually would do well to follow young Angelo's blueprint. Some examples from his journal include:

Daily: Devote at least a quarter of an hour to prayer upon waking up; de-

vote a quarter hour to spiritual reading; before dinner make an examination concerning ways to rid yourself of vices or failings replacing them
with virtues; read carefully and thoughtfully a whole chapter from The
Imitation of Christ by Thomas à Kempis.

Weekly: Confession; fast Friday and Saturday; on those days devote an extra
quarter of hour to prayer or spiritual reading, if possible, in the quiet of
some church; meet with the spiritual director for accountability.

Monthly: Ask one of the "most exemplary and zealous" spiritual friends to
observe your behavior and candidly but charitably identify any faults;
confer with the spiritual director about faults identified and the best way
to correct them.

Yearly: Go on retreat to do the spiritual exercises of Ignatius Loyola; before
going on a yearly vacation, consult with the spiritual director for sugges-
tions to use the time for spiritual profit."

Continuing his theological education, Roncalli was ordained
as a priest in August 1904 and assigned as secretary to the new
bishop of Bergamo. This appointment proved to be deeply formative for the young priest as the bishop was a spiritual visionary
deeply concerned about the poor and generating social reforms to
improve their condition. The bishop died in 1914 just as World
War I was erupting. With a change of diocesan leadership and the
beginning of the war, Roncalli saw those events as a time of transition in his own life. He resigned his post, enlisted into the Italian
army serving in both the medical corps and as a chaplain.

Because of his work with the bishop of Bergamo, Roncalli
came to the attention of his close friend, Pope Benedict XV. Thus,
when the war ended the pope asked Roncalli to direct the 1920
Eucharistic Congress to be hosted in Bergamo. This congress was
a major religious event in the Italian Catholic church, bringing
together tens of thousands of clergy, religious and lay people meeting for worship and prayer over several days. His skill at organiz-
ing and directing this massive event, as well as his skill at working
with hundreds of volunteers was noted by Vatican officials.

Four years later, Pope Pius XI established Vatican diplomatic
relations with Bulgaria, a nation predominantly Eastern Orthodox.
The pope asked Roncalli to be his representative (apostolic delegate) to Bulgaria and to emphasize the importance of his appointment, Pius XI made Roncalli a bishop in 1925.

All of this surprised Roncalli. In his journal he wrote: "I have not sought or desired this new ministry: the Lord has chosen me ... so it will be for him to cover up my failings and supply my insufficiencies.... This comforts me and gives me tranquility and confidence." Though he was now becoming an ecclesiastical official of considerable importance, Roncalli expressed his desire to remain spiritually focused and grounded. Shortly after accepting the appointment, he wrote in his journal: "I want to be all and wholly for God, penetrated with his light, shining with love for God and the souls of men.... In my new state of my life of prayer must take on a new aspect."

This diplomatic assignment was the first of several which would last three decades for Roncalli. In Bulgaria, Roncalli quickly realized his work was challenging. Because the state religion was Orthodox, his presence as the Vatican representative was viewed with suspicion by Bulgarian Orthodox clergy as well as some government leaders. However, the larger challenge in this appointment was working with the Vatican bureaucracy which caused serious difficulties for Roncalli. In his journal there is this cryptic entry: "I have been a bishop for 20 months. As I clearly foresaw, my ministry has brought me many trials. But, and this is strange, these are not caused by the Bulgarians for whom I work, but by the central organs of ecclesiastical administration. This is a form of mortification and humiliation that I did not expect and which hurts me deeply.... I must, I will accustom myself to bearing this cross with more patience, clam and inner peace than I have so far shown. I shall be particularly careful in what I say to anyone about this."

Though the population of Bulgaria was some seven million, there were only 50,000 Catholics. Roncalli visited and spoke at tiny Catholic parishes encouraging the faithful; however he responded to the needs of all Bulgarians. In a 1925 letter to his sister Ancilla he told of helping Bulgarian refugees returning home after ethnic violence: "The Holy Father has given me a hundred thousand lire for the poor refugees who are returning to Bulgaria from Greece or Serbia. With this sum I have begun to provide one meal a day for 250 of the poorest children.... If you could see the destitution here! And this is still the result of the war. Imagine what it would be like for us if we had been expelled from our own land and obliged to go wandering through the world, finding ourselves perhaps in Switzerland, in winter, without a roof over our heads and penniless, with old people and children in such weather."

After nine years in Bulgaria, Roncalli was appointed apostolic delegate to Turkey and Greece (1935) where, using his diplomatic skills, he was able to ease starvation in Greece. As war in Europe began to spread across countries, Greece was not spared. First, the Italians invaded in 1940 but were driven back by Greek forces. Because Italy was aligned with Germany, Hitler quickly ordered German troops to attack Greece supporting Italian forces. The result of these invading armies was a massive disruption in food production and delivery. The Greek population was starving and Roncalli became instrumental in getting food to starving Greeks by establishing a comfortable working relationship with Damaskinos, metropolitan of the Greek Orthodox church.

Damaskinos had succeeded in obtaining permission from Germany and Italy to have 370,000 tons of wheat sent to Greece from other countries. However, persuading the Allies to let food get through the blockade was a huge challenge because they feared the food would fall into enemy hands. When Damaskinos was asked by German authorities how he would contact the Allies' leaders, Damaskinos said: "I shall work with a Christian church with whom my own church was once united."

Upon learning of the metropolitan's plan, Roncalli stepped forward offering Damaskinos his services. This was a gracious act on Roncalli's part because in volunteering to help, he preserved the metropolitan's pride in not having to ask a Roman Catholic to help. During their private meeting, the metropolitan told Roncalli, "A thousand Greeks are dying every day of starvation. We must do something." To which Roncalli immediately responded: "We will!" Roncalli took a letter from Damaskinos addressed to Pius XII appealing for his aid in permitting food to be shipped into Greece and then personally delivered the letter to the pope adding his own urgent appeal. Those joint efforts of Roncalli and Damaskinos were successful in allowing tens of thousands of Greeks survive the famine.

In his role as apostolic delegate to Turkey and Greece, Roncalli was also instrumental in saving thousands of Jewish lives by launching "Operation Baptism." In early 1944, the American Jewish leader Ira Hirschmann requested an interview with Roncalli in Turkey. Hirschmann came prepared with statistics and eye-witness accounts of the Jewish plight in Hungary, pleading with Roncalli to help Jews in Turkey. After listening carefully, Roncalli proposed "Operation Baptism" explaining he knew of nuns in Budapest who had given baptismal certificates to Jews and that the Nazis recognized these, leaving the holders alone. Roncalli told Hirschmann he was prepared to make available as many baptismal certificates as were necessary, adding he had no vested interest in whether any Jews actually attended Mass or, when the war ended, remained in the church. His only concern was the saving of lives.

An exuberant and joyful Hirschmann returned to Washington saying: "The Catholic hierarchy, which enjoys a large influence in Hungary, took unusual spontaneous measures to rescue Jewish citizens wherever possible.... [I refer] to the baptism of thousands of Hungarian Jews in air raid shelters." Of course, Hirschmann was discreet and never revealed Roncalli as the source of those baptismal certificates.

Following the liberation of France in 1944, Roncalli was named Vatican representative to France and in 1953, Pope Pius XII made him a cardinal and patriarch of Venice. It was an appropriate appointment for a priest who served arduously and loyally for many decades. Roncalli was in his 72nd year and noted in his journal: "I am beginning my direct ministry at an age—72 years—when others end theirs.... In the few years I have still to live, I want to be a holy pastor.... Sometimes the thought of the short time left to me tempts me to slacken my efforts. But with God's help I will not give in. I neither fear to die nor refuse to live."

Believing that the position as cardinal of Venice would be his final service to the church, no one was more surprised than Roncalli when he was elected pope five years later in October, 1958. In fact, he even arrived at the Vatican for the consistory having purchased a return train ticket to Venice. Upon becoming pope, John continued in his determination to be truly a spiritual leader. A month after his election, he wrote: "Nothing has value for history and human life, nothing has any value for the church and for souls, unless the pontiff is holy in deed as well as in title."

Though his election was a surprise also to Catholics around the world, his warm pastoral style immediately began to attract attention and admiration. As he began his papacy, John not only maintained but heightened his pastoral concern, especially for the poor—some of whom worked directly for the Vatican. This reality came to his attention one day in 1959 when he saw an electrician doing some work on the grounds. Approaching the man, John asked "How are things going?" to which the electrician replied: "Badly, badly, your eminence." The man looked so weary, exhausted and depressed that John inquired further about the man, his family and his work. The electrician poured out the frustration of his struggle with poverty. "We'll have to do something about this," was the surprising response.

Shortly after that conversation John raised the pay of Vatican employees 25 to 40 percent. The employees being paid the least received the largest increase in wages. Explaining this change to Vatican administrators, John said: "We cannot always require others to observe the church's teaching on social justice if we do not apply it in our own domain. The church must take the lead in social justice by its own good example."

On December 25, 1958—a mere ten weeks after he came to the papal throne—John became the first pope since 1870 to make pastoral visits in his diocese of Rome. The first was to children infected with polio at the Bambino Gesu hospital. That was followed by a Christmas visit to prisoners at the ironically named "Queen of Heaven Prison in Rome". This pastoral call even astonished his staff who viewed it as highly irregular. Parts of the Queen of Heaven prison buildings dated back to 1654. It was the oldest, largest and most notorious prison in Rome. Addressing the large group of inmates who gathered to see him, John explained: "You could not come to me, so I came to you."

Though prison officials received little advance warning, they managed to map out a course for the Pope's visit by putting down a red carpet. Almost immediately, John veered off the runway, walking down gloomy and musty corridors. He arrived at one cell block where the most violent were confined and upon noticing that prisoners were still locked behind bars, said in his loudest voice: "Open the gates. Do not bar them from me. They are all children of our Lord."

While at the prison an old man with a lengthy prison record approached John confessing: "I have made many mistakes, Holy Father." Bending down to the kneeling man, John wiped his tears away, raised him and embraced him with a warm bear hug consoling the man with these words: "I looked into your eyes with my eyes. I have put my heart near your heart."

Some 1,000 prisoners assembled to meet and greet John, and he addressed them as "Dear sons and brothers," telling them his own brother had once been arrested and jailed for hunting without a license and that he understood why a man might break the law to steal for his hungry family.

His visit was a sensation not only among the inmates and prison officials, but with the media who were fascinated by a pope who visited a jail. Later, he wrote in his journal: "... great astonishment in the Roman, Italian and international press. I was hemmed in all sides: authorities, photographers, prisoners, wardens ..."

Because of his age at election—76—it was assumed he would merely be a transitional or "caretaker" pope. Though his reign was a brief five years, historians regard it as the most important pontificate since the Middle Ages due to his decision to call an ecumenical council of the universal church—the first since 1870 and only the 21st in the church's history. His aim in calling the council was to bring about a renewal of the church by having it adapt its organization and teaching to meet the needs of the modern world.

Unfortunately, John would not live to see the finish of his Vatican Council vision. From the start of the first session, his health began to diminish. Only those closest to him knew he was suffering from stomach cancer, but because of his age, surgery was deemed too risky. As a result, his health continued to decline. He appeared at his window overlooking St. Peter's Square for the last time on May 23, 1963. Shortly after that he reassured those around him: "My bags are packed and I am ready, very ready to go." Earlier he had mentioned this same readiness in a letter to his older brother Savero: "My 80 years of completed life tell me, as they tell you, dear Savero, that what is more important is always to keep ourselves well prepared for a sudden departure, because this is what matters most: to make sure of eternal life, trusting in the goodness of the Lord who sees all and makes provision for all."

Pope John XIII died quietly on June 3, 1963. The Vatican press office issued this final bulletin: "He suffers no more." Outside the papal window thousands in St. Peter's Square began to grieve along with millions around the world. Many times John XXIII came before groups saying, "I am your brother."

The world believed him!

Reflection: Wisdom from Pope John XXIII

Consult not your fears but your hopes and your dreams. Think not about your frustrations, but about your unfulfilled potential. Concern yourself not with what you tried and failed in, but with what it is still possible for you to do.

If God created shadows it was to better emphasize the light.

Women are gaining an increasing awareness of their natural dignity. Far from being content with a purely passive role or allowing themselves to be regarded as a kind of instrument, they are demanding both in domestic and in public life the rights and duties which belong to them as human persons.

Everything can be lost if people do not find some way to work together to save the peace.

My only wish is that my life should end in a holy manner. I tremble at the thought of having to bear pain, responsibilities, or difficulties beyond my poor capacity, but I trust in the Lord.

Holiness consists not in penances and extraordinary practices but in seeking in all things the Lord's will.

My children, love one another. Love one another, because this is the greatest commandment of the Lord.

God created men as brother's, not foes. They are to work in brotherly coöperation for the common prosperity of human society, not simply for their own particular goals.

Action: How to Be like Pope John XXIII

1. Live with a sacred optimism. John practiced a "cheerfulness at all times" and rejected voices of "those prophets of gloom, who are always forecasting disaster, as though the end of the world were at hand."

2. Ask others to pray for you. When it became known that John was to be made a cardinal, he wrote his family to share the news requesting: "Ask [God] to make me a good cardinal, a peace-loving and gentle cardinal." Whenever you face a difficult decision or a major life challenge ask those close to you for their prayers.

3. Curtail criticism. "See everything, overlook a great deal, correct a little," was John's philosophy. Curtail criticism. You'll be happier. So will your family and friends.

4. Practice self-restraint. Follow John's lead—"It is my nature to talk too much. A ready tongue is one of God's good gifts but it must be handled with care and respect, with moderation, so that I may be welcome and not found to be a bore."

5. Read biographies of spiritual lives. One of the best ways to deepen your own spiritual life is to read about others who are models of spirituality. Pope John loved St. Francis de Sales calling him "the gentlest of saints" and "a magnificent figure." He wrote: "I have read his life so many times!"

6. Practice what you preach. In all your relationships be a model of integrity by practicing what you preach. "I really must make sure that I never tell others to do what I do not try to practice myself," John noted in his journal.

7. **Be kind.** This was a lifelong goal of John's. "My dealing with others must always be marked with dignity, simplicity and kindness, a radiant and serene kindness."

8. **Observe yourself.** This "examination of conscience" was something John did all his life. From time to time, take a deep and honest look at yourself so any issues may be addressed before they enlarge. After one period of self-study John wrote: "Having made a general examination of my behavior during these recent days, I have found good reason to blush and feel humble."

9. **Remember: you are a role model.** We are visible to family, friends, colleagues, neighbors, acquaintances. Be a positive influence. That's the sentiment John expressed: "One learns Christian behavior in social and economic matters by actual Christian action in those fields."

10. **Don't take yourself so seriously.** A few days after he was elected pope, John's family were granted a special audience. The Roncallis entered the papal apartments timidly and nervously, dropping their gifts—peasant bread, ham and wine packed in brightly covered cloths tumbled to the floor. Their embarrassment was eased by John who smiled and said reassuringly: "Don't be afraid. It's only I." The lesson from John for us: Lighten up. Don't take yourself so seriously.

Books by Pope John XXIII

Journal of a Soul (This lifelong journal of Pope John XXIII, begun when he was 14 and ending with his death, is one of the world's finest spiritual autobiographies).

Books about Pope John XXIII

I Will Be Called John: A Biography of Pope John XXIII by Lawrence Elliott
Pope John XXIII by Thomas Cahill

10

Thea Bowman

Soulful Mystic

Sometimes people think they have to do big things in order to make change, but if each one would light a candle we'd have a tremendous light. —*Thea Bowman*

In 1954 a young woman entered a Catholic community—The Franciscan Sisters of Perpetual Adoration (FSPA)—in La Crosse, Wisconsin. At that time the evening-meal custom was to dine in silence while listening to a spiritual reading. That night, the person reading was an African-American woman. Because blacks and whites were generally separated and segregated then in the United States, the novice found herself thinking: "How interesting, the nuns have black people doing their reading." That initial impression is related by Charlene Smith, FSPA, who later discovered that the her Franciscan community did not have black servants and that the reader that evening was another Franciscan sister, Thea Bowman. As diverse as the Catholic church is worldwide, in the 1950s' United States it was still rare to find African-Americans as part of religious communities.

Bertha Bowman was born December 29, 1937, in Yazoo City, Mississippi, the only child of Theon Edward, a physician, and Mary Esther, a teacher. Bertha's grandfather was a slave. Her later calling to religious life may have had its roots in her father's example for Dr. Bowman had the potential to enjoy a successful profession as a physician in New York, but an aunt had suggested his skills might be better used serving the African-American community in Mississippi because blacks were denied medical care in the segregated south.

Soon after her birth, the family moved to Canton, Mississippi, a small community of 8,000—half of whom were African-American. The town was rigidly segregated. Whites had their streets and residential sections as did blacks. Except for shopping in stores owned and operated by whites, Bertha had no social contact with white people saying, "There was never a single white that I really knew." Because both parents were educated, they wanted the same for their daughter, but in the southern states African-American children received a very limited education, often ending at the fifth or sixth grade.

Though the family was Methodist, the best option for Bertha to receive an education was at a Catholic school, Holy Child Jesus in Canton. Even though they had some reservations about Catholicism, her parents nevertheless enrolled Bertha at this school in the sixth grade. It was administered by the Franciscan Sisters of Perpetual Adoration, an order specifically established for teaching African- American children.

This made an indelible impression upon young Bertha Bowman. Whereas southern whites dismissed blacks as inferior and immoral, the white Franciscan Sisters of Perpetual Adoration welcomed, embraced and loved her. "I was drawn to examine and accept the Catholic faith because of the day-to-day lived witness of Catholic Christians who first loved me, then shared with me their story, their values, their beliefs ... [and] then invited me to share with them in community prayer and mission," she later recalled. "As a child I did not recognize evangelization at work in my life. I did recognize love, service, community, prayer and faith."

In that welcoming and loving environment created by the sisters, Bertha thrived intellectually and spiritually. She excelled in her studies, joined the school choir, and was given a vision of a world larger than the cotton fields of Mississippi. It was not long before Bertha announced to her parents her desire to become a Catholic and to enter religious life. Initial parental resistance gave way to acceptance. In 1947 she was baptized along with another little boy. A few years later, at age 15 Bertha left Mississippi to join the Franciscan Sisters at their mother house in La Crosse, Wisconsin where she became the only African-American member at the St. Rose Convent. She was given the name "Thea" which means "of God." From then on Bertha was Sister Thea who brought along her African-American culture. One sister recalls: "It was a joy to sit beside her because her singing was so beautiful; she sang from her spirit."

Because of her inquisitive, grasping mind and love of children, her superiors felt the best use of her talents lay in becoming a teacher. Progressing successfully through the formative years required for religious life, Thea took final vows in 1963. In addition, she studied and graduated with a B.A. degree in English from Viterbo College in LaCrosse. She taught fifth and sixth grade in that city for two years and then was delighted to be assigned as a teacher at Holy Child Jesus in Canton. Thea returned home to teach at the same elementary school which was so formative in her own life. While there, her superiors encouraged her to continue graduate studies and in 1968 they sent her to the Catholic University of America in Washington, DC, where she earned a doctorate in English. This period coincided with the civil rights movement under the leadership of Martin Luther King, Jr., and the transformation of the nation regarding race.

On graduating, Thea returned to Wisconsin where from 1972 to 1978 she taught African-American literature and chaired the English department at Viterbo College. While there she founded and directed the "Hallelujah Singers" who became well known and highly popular for their singing of African-American spirituals, plus there was considerable demand for Thea to share her African-American heritage, particularly the music, so the "Hallelujah Singers" received invitations to perform throughout the United States.

In 1978 her order kindly transferred Thea home to Canton where she could care for her aging parents. She became the director of the Office of Intercultural Affairs for the diocese of Jackson, Mississippi, a position which gave her a platform to critique linger-

Eleven Mystics

ing racial prejudice while promoting cultural awareness and sensitivity. She was also a founding faculty member of the Institute for Black Catholic Studies (1980) at Xavier University of Louisiana in New Orleans.

Her years of experience and training combined with a prophetic vision allowed her to impact American Catholicism by providing an intellectual, spiritual, historical and cultural foundation for developing and legitimizing a distinct worship form for black Catholics. She explained: "When we understand our history and culture, then we can develop the ritual, the music, and the devotional expression that satisfy us in the church."

In 1987 Thea was instrumental in the publication of a seminal new African-American Catholic hymnal, *Lead Me, Guide Me: The African-American Catholic Hymnal*. James P. Lyke, OFM, PhD, the auxiliary bishop of Cleveland, coördinated the hymnal project because he felt it was born of the needs and aspirations of Black Catholics. Thea was actively involved in helping select songs to be included and it includes an essay by Thea: "The Gift of African-American Sacred Song" which said, "Black sacred song is soulful song," and then went on to describe it these five ways:

1. *holistic: challenging the full engagement of mind, imagination, memory, feeling, emotion, voice and body.*
2. *participatory: inviting the worshiping community to join in contemplation, in celebration and in prayer;*
3. *real: celebrating the immediate concrete reality of the worshiping community—grief or separation, struggle or oppression, determination or joy—bringing that reality to prayer within the community of believers;*
4. *spirit-filled: energetic, engrossing, intense;*
5. *life-giving: refreshing, encouraging, consoling, invigorating, sustaining.*

In her lectures, Thea frequently cited as an example the energetic and vital Catholic African-American congregation, Holy Ghost Parish, in Opelousas, Louisiana. With attendance of more than 3,000 people, it was one of the largest and most active black parishes in the nation. Services were led by a choir, readers, servers and a celebrant who "moved in rhythms held sacred for generations," she noted.

Thea argued this type of energetic worship should be received as a gift and a worship model which the wider Catholic community could consider and utilize. Little by little, Thea gained both respect and a national reputation among Catholic leaders, urging and persuading them to offer religious services which reflected different cultural styles of music and worship. She also modeled the diversity herself wearing African-style gowns, wearing her long hair in traditional braids. Through it all, Thea challenged the church to adapt itself culturally to various expressions in order to retain vitality and growth.

When invited to address the U.S. Catholic Bishops in June, 1989, Thea began her address by singing the black spiritual "Sometimes I Feel Like A Motherless Child," then proceeded to gently challenge the bishops to help her and other marginalized people find their rightful place within the church. She said to them: "What does it mean to be black and Catholic? It means that I come to my church fully functioning. That doesn't frighten you, does it? I come to my church fully functioning. I bring myself, my black self, all that I am, all that I have, all that I hope to become, I bring my whole history, my traditions, my experiences, my culture, my African-American song and dance and gesture and movement and teaching and preaching and healing and responsibility as gifts to the church." The Bishops were powerfully and visibly moved by Thea and applauded her. When she finished speaking, they stood, linking arms and singing as Thea led them in the spiritual, "We Shall Overcome."

As the meeting ended, the bishops presented Thea with a dozen roses which she proudly held in the air proclaiming: "I accept these roses in memory of all the women who have nurtured you into the episcopacy." The Bishops applauded her once again and later one commented, "At a time of much division in the church, Sister Thea possess the charismatic gifts to heal, to bring joy to the church. She had no time for useless, destructive arguments. She was too busy celebrating life."

Throughout her life, Thea affirmed and built on her African-

American spiritual roots. One of those foundations was Scripture. She said, "God was so alive in my world. I was reared around a lot of old people. They knew Scripture. I knew people who could not read or write, but they could quote you Scripture with the chapter and verse. They would use Scripture when they were tired and a Scripture when they were frustrated, a Scripture to challenge us,... a Scripture to threaten you, a Scripture to reward you or to praise you or to teach you: I grew up in that kind of world."

Of course, African-American songs were instrumental in her spiritual formation as well. She shared her insights on the spiritual, "Joshua Fit De Battle of Jericho," saying: "There were no weapons, no M-16s, no bombs. There was no need for violence. The battle was in God's hands. God commanded Joshua and the people to encircle Jericho with music, ritual and celebration. God command-ed the people to shout—One Lord, one faith, one united people—and the wall came tumbling down. The power of God and the power of a united, believing people prevailed."

Ultimately, it was the joy and love of the Franciscan sisters which impacted her soul, prompting her to become a Catholic and joining their order. In turn, she came to love the liturgy and spiri-tuality of Catholicism. Yet, it was her encounter with white reli-gious sisters which opened the window of her soul. Through their lives she saw white Christians who "preached" love, not hatred, unity not division.

Years later, in a television interview in Wisconsin, Thea spoke glowingly of the "Catholic Christians" who came to work with her people. "Catholic Christians came into my community and they helped us with education; they helped us with health care; they helped us to find our self-respect and to realize our capabili-ties when the world had told us for so long that we were nothing and would amount to nothing. And I wanted to be part of that effort. That's radical Christianity, that's radical Catholicism."

Throughout her entire life, she never forgot the kindness of her Franciscan sisters and that she was one of them. "I am a Fran-ciscan," she declared. "I want to be an instrument of peace. I want to be an instrument of hope. I want to be an instrument of faith and joy."

In 1984, Thea was diagnosed with cancer and began a six-year struggle. Despite the debilitating effects of treatment, illness and confinement to a wheelchair, Thea continued to be the main African-American spokesperson for the church to heighten its intercultural and interracial awareness. During those six years, her prayer was simple but profound: "Lord, let me live until I die. If that prayer is answered, how long really doesn't matter."

As her health deteriorated, appreciation and love for Thea flowed in from her many friends and admirers. One example of this took place when she was confined to bed and barely clinging to life. Forty members of the Hallelujah Singers came to see her and crammed into the living room of her Mississippi home to sing gospel songs. There was emotional good-bye from her and as they left the choir director casually mentioned the group was planning to stop at a local McDonalds. They were seated for a meal when they noticed a car pull into the parking lot. A frail Sister Bowman was in the back seat. Spontaneously, the group left the restaurant, surrounded the car singing "Deep River" because they knew it was one of Thea's favorite spirituals.

At the young age of 52, Thea, the granddaughter of a slave who became a Catholic sister, died in Canton on March 30, 1990. Tributes were paid to Thea from all over the country. In New York, Cardinal O'Connor devoted his column to her in his diocesan newspaper writing: "Friedrich Nietzsche said 'The world no longer believes because believers no longer sing'. He didn't know Sister Thea Bowman, dark nightingale. I am grateful that I did."

On April 4, Thea was buried next to her parents in Elmwood Cemetery, Memphis, Tennessee. The words she requested to be engraved on her white tombstone were these: "SHE TRIED."

Reflection: Wisdom from Thea Bowman

I can't preach in the church. Women can't preach in the Catholic church. But I can preach in the streets. I can preach in the neighborhood. I can preach in the home. I can teach and preach in the family.

The gift you have becomes a gift to humanity.

Maybe I'm not called to make big changes in the world, but if I have somehow helped or encouraged somebody along the journey, then I've done what I'm called to do.

I know in faith I am weak and God is strong, and he can accept my poor efforts.

Let us resolve to make this week holy by sharing holy peace and joy within our families, sharing family prayer on a regular basis, making every meal a holy meal where loving conversations bond family members in unity.

If we are not family, we can't become church.

As we journey together in faith and hope and love, we have got to hold on to one another. You have got to believe in the essential goodness of all humanity/

My goal is to share good news. I want people to know that happiness is possible.

It has to be love—love that overcomes fear, that shares and makes us sure that nobody is hungry—that unites us.

Action: How to Be like Thea Bowman

1. Help the poor. No matter how little you may have, there is always someone who has even less that you. Reach out to those who are the poorest of the poor. Be like the gentle and kind Franciscan sisters who came to Mississippi instilling love, dignity and hope.

2. Let your light shine. Jesus was concerned that people with light would hesitate to let it shine because of timidity or cowardice or some other reason: "You are the light of the world.... Let your light shine" (Mt 5:14,16 NIV). Thea built on this teaching of Jesus saying: "Let your light shine. Each one teach one. Walk your talk. You didn't get your light only to sit on it."

3. Sing. Even if you can't hold a tune, sing aloud to yourself.

Studies reveal that music has the power to heal. This was something Thea knew. "When I hurt I like to sing some of the old songs. I find that prayer and song can take me beyond the pain."

4. Laugh. Even though Thea struggled with a terminal illness she found "laughter to be helpful, so I laugh.

5. Be someone's bridge over troubled water. White Franciscan sisters came to a poor black community in Mississippi bringing love and hope. They became Thea's, and many other persons', bridge over the troubled waters of segregation. When someone is in need, respond in any way that you can.

6. Never, never give up. Though Thea's cancer could not be contained nor put in remission and even though she lived with constant pain she said: "I grew up with people who believed you could serve the Lord from a sickbed or a deathbed."

7. Offer God whatever you have for service. Many people feel they don't have enough talent to make a difference. God can multiply talents. Thea was amazed to discover "God [is] using me beyond my comprehension. God has given me the grace to see some of the seeds I've sown bear good fruit, and I am so grateful."

8. Appreciate and celebrate multiculturalism. If your faith community is primarily made up of one ethnic group, be sure to welcome "outsiders" when they attend and make them feel like "insiders." Thea asked: "Can you see yourself in a church where there are people who are black, where there are people who are white, where there are people who are brown, where there are people who are of Asian heritage?"

9. Be part of community building. People need people. We need each other for encouragement, personal growth and spiritual evolution. Thea reminds us to do our part in community building: "Everybody needs family. We start with a basic human need for family and for one another. We realized that one father, one mother are not enough: that families need the support of other families, and so we seek ways of bonding, nourishing, healing."

10. Become involved in your faith community. It needs you. Work with others to make a difference. Thea said, "It takes a whole church to raise a child."

Eleven Mystics

Books by Thea Bowman

Thea Bowman: In My Own Words
Sister Thea Bowman, Shooting Star: Selected Writings and Speeches

11

Eknath Easwaran

Inter-religious Mystic

*The great mystics go through life without fuss and frenzy as
if they had all the time in the world, and their lives seem so
much richer than ours that we have to stop and wonder why.*
—*Eknath Easwaran*

In 1959 Eknath Easwaran, a young Indian scholar and teacher
of Victorian literature, received a Fulbright Exchange Scholarship
giving him an opportunity to study and teach in the United States.
That travel involved two ocean liners: the first was an aging ship
which had been in service before the first world war. Though it
was completely without luxuries, Easwaran enjoyed the passengers
"from empire builders to scholars from the Far East."

As they traveled across the Arabian Sea, monsoon storms
struck, tossing the ship like a small toy boat. He recalled how
frightening it was as he clung, with other passengers, to the ship's
rails. "A storm is a great equalizer. All distinctions of class and
color were swept away," he said. Everyone cheered with relief
when the storm passed, but the ship was badly damaged and had
to dock for repairs.

A second ship, *The Queen Mary*, took him from Europe to
America which was an utterly different experience. When the
Queen Mary hit rough seas on the Atlantic, "we sailed through
majestically without a roll," he remembers. Curious, he asked why
the ship was not tossed about in the storm and learned from an

officer that it had been installed with stabilizers so "now the rough waters don't bother her at all."

Easwaran often told that story in his talks to illustrate an important spiritual truth. Like a storm at sea, "life is a great equalizer ... regardless of class, color, status, birth or wealth, some of us sail through surely while others flounder and even go under." He would remind audiences that most people are not born with the innate skill to successfully weather life's storms. Yet, everyone could acquire the necessary skills. "We can't control the weather outside, but we can control how we respond. Like the *Queen Mary*, we can install stabilizers—in the mind. For it is in the mind that the storms of life really blow.... The steadiness of mind is one of the most practical of skills. Without it, no one can face the challenges of life without breaking."

From his arrival to the United States in 1959 until his death in 1999, Easwaran emerged as a persuasive and popular teacher of spirituality and was instrumental in reawakening an interest in the spiritual for Westerners from all walks of life.

Easwaran was born in southern Indian state of Kerala in 1910 and raised by his mother and grandmother whom he would consistently honor as his "guru." In the book, *The Making of A Teacher: Eknath Easwaran*, he explained this woman's influence over him to authors Tim and Carol Flinders: "My grandmother's life was a mirror of the divine splendor of the Lord, the love and wisdom that lie within us. It was all I needed. That is why our tradition maintains that even if all the scriptures were lost, we could reconstruct them from the life of just one illumined man or woman. It would be sufficient."

His grandmother, lacking in formal education but rich in spirituality, was a powerful example of someone who had a constant awareness of God. She taught him that spirituality is immensely practical because it was something to be lived out day-by-day in the presence of family and within the wider community.

His early education took place in the village school until he was 16 when the left to attend a nearby Catholic college. There he acquired a profound appreciation of Christian saints and mystics.

Easwaran did graduate studies at the University of Nagpur in English literature and law, and on graduating, he served as a professor of literature at the same university.

Though he loved academia and his students, Easwaran experienced his own dark night of the soul which would propel his life into a completely different direction. It was precipitated by the death of his beloved grandmother who died the same year Gandhi was assassinated (1947). Easwaran had met and spent time with Gandhi and was deeply impacted by Gandhi's spirituality.

The loss of two spiritual mentors threw him into a personal and professional crisis. "I was already well-launched on a career as a professor of English literature.... I was quite content with the satisfactions of writing and of sharing my passionate love of English and Sanskrit literature with responsive students," he recalled. "All those things that had promised such satisfaction turned to ashes. Books that had fascinated me for decades ceased to speak to my condition," he said. At that point, he began to turn inward and take up the practice of meditation.

While dealing with his internal crisis, he continued teaching. In 1959, he came as a Fulbright scholar to the University of Berkeley, California where he began introducing meditation to people in the Bay Area. After a return to India, Easwaran decided to come back to America because he found audiences remarkably receptive to him and his spiritual teachings. He returned in 1965 and resumed teaching at Berkeley where he taught what is believed to be the first certified course on meditation offered at a major American University.

In order to spread his ideas to wider audiences, Easwaran established the Blue Mountain Center of Meditation as well as Nilgiri Press, a small publishing branch of the meditation center, which began to publish Easwaran's lectures and books. He is best known for teaching "passage meditation" which involves taking a spiritual text, memorizing it and then repeating slowly, word by word, during a time of meditation. The text serves not only as a mantra focusing the mind, but the repetition permits the text to deeply penetrate our being. Easwaran calls such spiritual texts "inspired words [which] can change us from the inside out." Passage meditation can be used by anyone.

Easwaran says: "The method of meditation presented here can be followed equally well in any religion or in none. I think that is the real secret of its appeal. It belongs to no movement, asks for no change of beliefs: it simply allows you to take the ideals you respond to and gradually, gracefully, makes them part of your character and your life."

Easwaran draws from the world religions for passage meditation. Some examples include a Christian passage meditation from St. Patrick:

Christ Be With Me
May the wisdom of God instruct me,
the eye of God watch over me,
the ear of God hear me,
the word of God give me sweet talk,
the hand of God defend me,
the way of God guide me.
Christ be with me.
Christ before me.
Christ after me.
Christ in me.
Christ under me.
Christ over me.
Christ on my right hand.
Christ on my left hand.
Christ on this side.
Christ on that side.
Christ at my back.

Another Christian passage meditation is from St. Theresa of Avila

You Are Christ's Hands
Christ has no body now on earth but yours,
no hands but yours,
no feet but yours.
Yours are the eyes through which is to look out
Christ's compassion to the world.
Yours are the feet with which he is to go about doing good.
Yours are the hands with which he is to bless people now.

Psalms figure largely in Easwaran's recommendations of spiritual texts—Psalm 23, 24 and 100. Having attended a Catholic college in India, Easwaran came to know and appreciate Christian saints. Thus he recommends for passage meditation, readings from saints such as Augustine, Anselm, Catherine of Genoa, Francis de Sales, Ignatius of Loyola, Francis of Assisi, Patrick—and many others.

Easwaran appreciates the depth of spirituality found in all the world's religions and cites passage meditations from Native American, Hindu, Christian, Buddhist, Jewish and the Tao. For the meditation to have an impact, an individual uses a passage which is personally meaningful, one with which they are able to bond spiritually. "The secret of [passage] meditation is simple," Easwaran says. "You become what you meditate on. When you use an inspirational passage every day in meditation, you are driving the words deep into your consciousness. Eventually they become an integral part of your personality, which means they will find constant expression in what you do, what you say and what you think."

Doing passage meditation is a simple process, but one which can produce profound results. A person sets some quiet time aside, as little as five minutes. Sitting in a comfortable position with back, neck and hands gently erect in a straight line, the individual then closes the eyes, breathes deeply and softly while silently reciting the words of the passage.

Easwaran describes passage meditation this way: "In the method of meditation I teach, the mind goes slowly through the words of a memorized inspirational passage like the Prayer of St. Francis, which begins, 'Lord, make me an instrument of they peace.' When the mind wanders—as it surely will—you simply bring it back to the words, giving them more attention. As concentration deepens, the words sink deep into consciousness and become an integral part of our character and conduct. Whatever passage is selected, it is important that the recitation be done slowly, permitting each inspiring word to drop like a jewel into the depths of your consciousness." By giving them full attention, the

meaning sinks in producing positive developments in the individual's life.

Along with passage meditation, Easwaran developed his Eight
Point Program for spiritual growth which are elaborated in his
book *Meditation: A Simple Eight Point Program for Translating
Spiritual Ideals into Daily Life*. In summary, these are:

1. *Meditation:* silent repetition of an inspirational passage from
one of the world's great religions. He recommended doing this for
a half hour each morning.

2. *Mantra recitation:* silent repetition of a sacred word or
phrase from one of the world's great religions. This was to be
recited off and on throughout the day.

3. *Slowing down:* reducing stress and frenzy by setting priori-
ties.

4. *One pointed attention:* being completely mindful to whatever
or whoever is at hand.

5. *Training the senses:* cultivating the self-discipline of enjoying
simple pleasures while avoiding cravings and unhealthy excesses.

6. *Putting others first:* gaining freedom from selfishness and
finding joy in helping others.

7. *Spiritual fellowship:* practicing meditation with a group of
people for mutual support and inspiration.

8. *Spiritual reading:* deepening personal spirituality by reading
inspirational works from the world's great religions.

Mantra use is an important aspect of Easwaran's spirituality.
While mantras have always been used in the Eastern religions,
their value became evident to Easwaran when he discovered that
the Christian tradition also employed mantras. Calling it a "simple
skill," he noted that a mantra was employed by St. Francis of
Assisi who constantly repeated "My God and my all." Easwaran
taught that mantra use was highly effective in stress reduction. For
that to take place, it is important to recite the mantra as often as
possible. "Whenever you get a moment free, unless you are doing
something that requires attention, repeat your mantra to yourself
silently, in the mind—while waiting, walking, washing dishes and
especially when falling asleep at night. Constant repetition drives

the mantra deep into consciousness, where it can anchor your mind so surely that no amount of agitation can sweep you away.... This is how we can gradually extend sovereignty over the mind."

Easwaran's popularity with Westerners lay in his practical and user-friendly spirituality. One example is found in his book, *Words to Live By*, where he expounds on the meaning of this Islamic proverb: "The words of the tongue should have three gatekeepers." Easwaran says that before a word leaves the mouth, the first gatekeeper asks: "Is this true?" Normally, this will "stop a lot of traffic immediately." However, if the word gets beyond the first gatekeeper, then the second one asks: "Is it kind?" If what is about to be said qualifies as kind, then the last gatekeeper asks: "Is it necessary?"

Easwaran readily admits that with these three gatekeepers on guard most of us would find very little to say. Then he adds: "I think it is necessary to make exceptions in the interests of good company and let the third gatekeeper look the other way now and then. After all, a certain amount of pleasant conversation is part of the artistry of living. But the first two gatekeepers should always be on duty."

Another contribution made by Easwaran was his translation and commentary of Hindu and Buddhist texts. Because he was raised in British India and lived in America, Easwaran was successful in making ancient Eastern teachings accessible and applicable to Westerners. His gift for bringing out the universality and timelessness of Eastern teachings was noted by Huston Smith, a highly respected scholar of world religions: "No one in modern times is more qualified—no, make that 'as qualified'—to translate the epochal *Classics of Indian Spirituality* than Eknath Easwaran. And the reason is clear: It is impossible to get to the heart of those classics unless you live them, and he did live them. My admiration of the man and his works is boundless."

Easwaran died in 1999. Fortunately, he left behind a large body of manuscripts which are gradually being published by Nilgiri Press permitting his practical spirituality to continue impacting future generations.

Reflection: Wisdom from Eknath Easwaran

The present is all we have. If we feel we don't have enough time, the first thing to do is not throw it away.

The widest possibilities for spiritual growth lie in the give-and-take of everyday relationships.

By virtue of being human, each of us has the capacity to choose, to change, to grow.

We have surrounded ourselves with such a bleak picture of who we are and what the world is.... Only by turning away from unreality— from negativity and separateness—will we begin to see and build a world that's not only sustainable but nourished and helps us realize our deepest longings for peace.

We all need joy, and we can all receive joy in only one way, by adding to the joy of others.

Patience can't be acquired overnight. It is just like building up a muscle. Every day you need to work on it.

The very pressure of time is an illusion. If we could slow the mind down, we would see that past and future have no reality. There is never any moment but the present, never any time but now.

What we do in meditation is to remove the obstacles that hide and cover our native capacity to love.

Action: How to Be like Eknath Easwaran

1. Meditate. Set aside time to still the mind. Even a few minutes a day can make a large difference. "Meditation is a kind of glass-bottom boat for observing the mind," says Easwaran.

2. Slow down. Ask yourself, "Why am I constantly busy and battling the clock? What's the point?" Live by this reminder from Easwaran: "A slower life ... is more effective, more artistic, much richer than a life lived as a race against the clock. It gives you time to pause, to think, to reflect, to decide, to weigh pros and cons. It give you time for relationships."

3. Be cheerful. Practice this even when the task at hand is one you may dislike. One reason Easwaran was always popular with students was his cheerful nature. He noted that being an English professor was sometimes "plain drudgery" and he cited having to read "150 freshman essays on Romeo and Juliet and marking the same misspellings over and over." Yet, he did not permit the drudgery to dampen his cheerfulness.

4. Grow through the darkness. Everyone experiences challenging times when life seems dim and dark. Easwaran experienced this with the death of his grandmother and the assassination of Gandhi. Be patient, as he was, giving the darkness time to recede. New growth will emerge for you as it did for Easwaran.

5. Practice compassion to all creatures. Easwaran reminded people: "Be compassionate to our fellow creatures recognizing that the same Self lives in them as in us."

6. Work to reduce your anger. This takes intentional effort and great personal discipline. When we reduce and eradicate anger "the result is the precious capacity to return love for abuse."

7. Use things but love people. In viewing our culture, Easwaran was alarmed to see how easily we love things but use people. Reverse this trend whenever you see it in yourself.

8. Practice selfless action. Whatever you do for others, free yourself from any selfish motives. Expect nothing in return when you help another person. Easwaran cautioned: "Work can benefit others and still carry a substantial measure of ego involvement. It may benefit others, but it will not necessarily benefit the doer. Everything depends on the state of mind."

9. Learn from saintly people wherever you encounter them. Easwaran loved and learned from Catholic saints, Sufi mystics, Buddhist visionaries, Hindu ascetics and Taoist sages.

10. Always be a person of hope. No matter how difficult and depressing things seem around the world, hold on to hope. "I am filled with hope for the coming decades," Easwaran often said. "I have been privileged to witness—in my own life and the lives of people close to me—just how much any human being can change."

Books by Eknath Easwaran

Passage Meditation: Bringing the Deep Wisdom of the Heart into Daily Life.

Timeless Wisdom: Passages for Meditation from the World's Saints and Sages

Words to Live By: A Daily Guide to Living an Exceptional Life

Additional copies of this book may be obtained
from your bookstore
or by contacting
Hope Publishing House
P.O. Box 60008
Pasadena, CA 91116 - U.S.A.
(626) 792-6123 / (800) 326-2671
Fax (626) 792-2121
HopePublishingHouse@gmail.com
www.hope-pub.com